The Book of Jubilees

Start Publishing PD LLC
Copyright © 2024 by Start Publishing PD LLC

All rights reserved, including the right to reproduce this book or portions thereof in any form whatsoever.

Start Publishing PD is a registered trademark of Start Publishing PD LLC
Manufactured in the United States of America

Cover art: Shutterstock/Taisiya Kozorez

Cover design: Jennifer Do

10 9 8 7 6 5 4 3 2 1

ISBN 979-8-8809-1357-2

The Book of Jubilees

translated by R. H. Charles

The Book of Jubilees, or, as it is sometimes called, "the little Genesis," purports to be a revelation given by God to Moses through the medium of an angel ("the Angel of the Presence," i. 27), and containing a history, divided up into jubilee-periods of forty-nine years, from the creation to the coming of Moses. Though the actual narrative of events is only carried down to the birth and early career of Moses, its author envisages the events of a later time, and in particular certain events of special interest at the time when he wrote, which was probably in the latter years of the second century B.C., perhaps in the reign of the Maccabean prince John Hyrcanus. Though distinguished from the Pentateuch proper ("the first Law," vi. 22), it presupposes and supplements the latter. The actual narrative embraces material contained in the whole of Genesis and part of Exodus. But the legal regulations given presuppose other parts of the Pentateuch, especially the so-called "Priest's Code" (P), and certain details in the narrative are probably intended to apply to events that occurred in the author's own time (the latter years of the second century B.C.). The author himself seems to have contemplated the speedy inauguration of the Messianic Age, and in this respect his point of view is similar to that of the Apocalyptic writers. But his work, though it contains one or two passages of an apocalyptic character, is quite unlike the typical apocalypses. It is largely narrative based upon the historical narratives in Genesis and Exodus, interspersed with legends, and emphasizing certain legal practices (such as the strict observance of the Sabbath, circumcision, etc.), and laying much stress upon their eternal obligation. But his main object was to inculcate a reform in the regulation of the calendar and festivals, in place of the intercalated lunar calendar, which he condemns in the strongest language. He proposes to substitute for this a solar calendar consisting of 12 months and containing 364 days. The result of such a system is to make all festivals, except the Day of Atonement, fall on a Sunday; the author also fixes the date of the Feast of Weeks (Pentecost) on Sivan 15th (in place of the traditional Sivan 6th). He obviously believes that the prevailing system has produced grave consequences in religious practice. The proper observance of the feasts, which had been prescribed by divine authority, is, according to his view, rendered impossible so long as the right principles for regulating the calendar are ignored. These principles are justified from the written Law, and are represented as having been ordained in heaven. To what party or tendency in Judaism did the author belong? Various answers have been given to this question, which will be fully discussed below. It is very difficult to believe, as Dr. Charles contends, that the author was a Pharisee, for the positions he advocates are in many respects fundamentally opposed to later Pharisaic practice. In particular, how can any member of the Pharisaic party, which from its beginning championed popular religious custom, have advocated a solar calendar? More can be said for the view that the author was a member of the Hasidim or "pious" (who must not be confounded with the Pharisees), while in a recent important discussion Leszynsky has made out a strong, if not quite convincing, case for Sadducean authorship. The Book has sometimes been styled a Midrash, but such a descriptive term needs some qualification. It claims to be a revelation, and not a mere exposition of Genesis and Exodus. At the same time, there is a certain Midrashic tendency observable in the way the author rewrites the older narratives, which reminds one of the work of the Chronicler as compared with the earlier canonical books which he remodelled. But Jubilees is not at all like the typical Midrash of the later Rabbinical period; it is more independent, and resembles rather such works as the "Chronicles of Jerahmeel," or the earlier (narrative) part of the "Apocalypse of Abraham."

The Book, which was probably composed in Hebrew, is divided into fifty chapters, and appears to be complete.

The Special Aims and General Character of the Book

It is obvious that Jubilees is dominated by certain interests and antipathies. It is to a large extent polemical in character, and its author desires at once to protest against certain tendencies which, in his view, threaten true religion, and to inculcate certain reforms. Incidentally it commends certain religious practices, and endeavours to invest them with enhanced sanctions. In the forefront, as its name ("the Book of Jubilees") suggests 2 stands the question of the Calendar. It is all important in the author's view that the divinely ordained principle according to which history is divided up by year-weeks (i. e. periods of 7 years) and jubilees (i. e. periods of 7 X 7 years) is recognized (Cf. i. 26 f.). Accordingly, he gives a history from Creation to Moses, in which the sequence of events is recorded and dated exactly by jubilee-periods, or portions of such. This leads up to a final section in which the law respecting jubilees and sabbatical years is solemnly enjoined. The writer's aim seems to have been nothing less than a reformation of the Jewish Calendar. The prevailing system has led to the nation "forgetting" new moons, festivals, and sabbaths (and (?) jubilees); in other words, it has produced grave irregularities in the observance of matters which were of divine obligation.

A cardinal feature of the writer's system is the jubilee-period, which consists of 7 X 7 (i. e. 49) years. Here we are confronted with a difficulty. The passage in Lev. (xxv. 8-14) which ordains the observance of the jubilee-year expressly identifies this, in the present form of the text, with the fiftieth year (Lev. xxv. 10 and 11). But it is incredible that the author of our Book would deliberately have violated the express injunctions of the Pentateuch on such a matter, and we are driven to conclude that he had a text before him in which the word "fiftieth" was absent. The wording of verses 8 and 9 is ambiguous, and allows of the explanation that the jubilee-year was the forty-ninth and not the fiftieth. It is quite possible that in verses 10 and 11 "fiftieth" has been added to the text, in the interests of the rival explanation that ultimately prevailed, for, as has been pointed out already, our Book presupposes a text of the Pentateuch that is independent of and earlier than M.T. This explanation suffers from the difficulty that the LXX and other ancient versions (including the Samaritan text) support the currently received reading. But it is not improbable that on such a matter the influence of Orthodox views may have operated to bring their text of the verses into harmony with the currently accepted theory.

But more revolutionary is the writer's advocacy of a solar calendar. In ii. 9 he says, "God appointed the sun to be a great sign upon the earth for days and for sabbaths, and for feasts and for years and for jubilees and for all seasons of the years." In Gen. i. 14 this function is assigned to the sun and the moon; but in our Book the moon is deliberately excluded. The writer objected fiercely to the traditional calendar which was based upon the changes of the moon, and was adjusted to the solar year by means of intercalation. How can his apparent violation of the express wording of Scripture be explained? His answer would probably have been that the solar year of 364 days (cf. vi. 32) was actually the system implied in the Pentateuch. It has been pointed out by Bacon that in the P sections of the Flood-narrative in Genesis a year of 364 days is pre-supposed. It is said that the Flood began on the 17th day of the second month, and ended on the 27th day of the second month the following year, i. e. reckoning by the ordinary lunar months, 12 months (= 12 X 29½ days) or 354 days + 10 days (to make up the solar year), or 364 days in all, this completing the one whole year which, according to the Babylonian source, was the length of the Flood's duration. Thus the author of Jubilees had a dogmatic basis within the text of the Pentateuch itself for his view that the true year was a solar one of 364 days. He may very well have believed that whatever may be the exact significance of Gen. i. 14, it could not override this fact. It is interesting to notice that this tradition of a solar year of 364 days should be implicit in the P sections of Genesis. There are strong reasons for believing that the author of Jubilees was a priest, and, as such, may have been acquainted in some special way with this priestly tradition. There are, however, difficulties in connexion with the reckoning of such a solar year. It is obvious that a year of 12 months, each of which contains 30 days, will only yield a total of 360 days. It has been supposed that our author overcame this difficulty by inserting one intercalary day at the beginning of each quarter. Thus each three months would contain 31 + 30 + 30 (= 91) days. But this solution will not harmonize with the date assigned by our author to the Feast of

Weeks, which is the "middle" of the third month (xvi. 13). Scholars are agreed that the 15th of Sivan is meant. Now the Feast of Weeks was to be celebrated on the fiftieth day, counting from the "morrow" after the Sabbath of Passover (Lev. xxiii. 15 f.). The Pharisees, as is well known, interpreted "Sabbath" here to be the first day of the Feast (Nisan 15th), whatever the day of the week on which it fell, and reckoned from Nisan 16th, which would bring the Feast of Weeks to Sivan 6th. Another view, with which our Book agrees, interpreted "sabbath" as = "week" (as in fact it has this meaning throughout the rest of the verse). Then render: And ye shall count unto you from the morrow after the (festival) week, from the day that ye bring the wave-sheaf, seven complete weeks shall there be, until the morrow after the seventh week ye shall number fifty days: the festival-week would be Nisan 15-21, and its "morrow" Nisan 22; reckoning 28 days to the month, this would leave 6 days in Nisan + 28 days in Iyar + 15 in Sivan = 49 +Nisan 22 = 50 (lays. This seems to have been the reckoning of our author. Moreover, since the year he advocates contains 364 days, the festivals would always fall upon the same day of the week, and as Nisan 1st the first day of Creation fell, according to his scheme, on the first day of the week, i. e. Sunday, it must always fall on that day; thus Nisan 14th and 21st would always fall on a Sabbath, while Nisan 22nd and Sivan 15th would always fall on a Sunday. To make the Feast of Weeks fall on the 1st day of the week was a Sadducean practice, and one that it is inconceivable that any Pharisee can ever have sanctioned or tolerated. It will be noticed, however, that the view of our author, according to which the Feast of Weeks falls on Sivan 15th, implies a reckoning of 28 days to the months Nisan and Iyar. How is this to be reconciled with a solar year of 12 months? Eppstein supposes that our author used two reckonings, one for the civil year of 12 months, 8 of 30, and 4 of 31 days, and an ecclesiastical year of 13 months each containing 28 days. But it is difficult to believe that the writer used two systems side by side. A better solution would be that he added a week to every third month, which would make each 3 months consist of 28 + 28 + 35 days (total 91 days), or 4 + 4 + 5 weeks. It is evident that his calendar-system is based upon the number 7; thus each month consists of 4 X 7 (or 5 X 7) days, while the year consists of 52 X 7 days, the year-week of 7 years, and the jubilee of 7 X 7 years. On this reckoning the Feast of Weeks would still fall on the 15th of Sivan, but the 15th would not strictly be the "middle" of that month, which, ex hypothesi, consisted of 35 days. It might, however, be used loosely for such a date. Perhaps, too, the author desired to avoid specifying more particularly this date, because current Sadducean practice (based upon 4 different length of days assigned to the months) would not quite harmonize with it. 1 With regard to the Passover, it is noticeable that our author interprets the phrase "between the two evenings" (at which time the Passover lamb was to be slain, cf. Exod. xii. 6; Lev. xxiii. 5) to mean the third part of the day (xlix. 10); i. e. assuming the day to contain 12 hours, we may fix the third part as from 2 to 6 p.m. This, again, contradicts Pharisaic practice. Notable, too, is the mention of wine in connexion with the Passover: All Israel was eating the flesh of the Paschal lamb and drinking the wine (xlix. 6). Now this was a Pharisaic custom in later times, and has no basis, apparently, in the canonical account in Exodus. In view, however, of the fact that our author usually follows the prescriptions of Scripture with scrupulous care, the question arises whether he did not, in fact, derive this from the Pentateuch. Leszyrisky suggests that the word rendered "bitter herbs" in Exod. xii. 8 ("with bitter herbs shall they eat it") was interpreted by our author to mean "wine"--the word simply means "bitter," or "what is poisonous," and a cognate form is used in connexion with wine in Deut. xxxii. 32. It is certainly curious that our author makes no mention of "bitter herbs" in connexion with the Egyptian Passover.

The Feast of Tabernacles, too, as described in our Book (xvi. 10-31), has certain peculiar features. In particular, the specifically Pharisaic custom of pouring water on the altar 2 at the Feast is not mentioned or recognized. Now as early as the time of Alexander Jannæus (102-76 B.C.) the Pharisees tried to enforce the adoption of this custom upon the Sadducean priest-king, who, to show his contempt, allowed the water, which should have been poured solemnly on the altar, to run over his feet. The protest that ensued was followed later by a massacre of Pharisees. It is difficult to believe that our author, a few years earlier, if he was himself a Pharisee, could have been ignorant of this custom, which was based upon old popular tradition. His silence concerning it is much more probably deliberate. The custom was objectionable, from the Sadducean standpoint, because it had no basis in the written Law. The custom of wearing wreaths upon the head which is here prescribed (xvi. 30) is also unknown to tradition; nor has it, apparently, any Scriptural basis, unless it was inferred as an act of rejoicing, from the words "and ye shall rejoice before the Lord your God seven days" (Lev. xxiii. 40), taken in conjunction with the command (in the preceding clause) to take "branches of palm trees, and boughs of thick trees, and willows of the brook." Wearing a wreath of palm-leaves may have been regarded as one of the ways in which this command was to be fulfilled

Even more striking are the sections which give directions about the observance of the Sabbath (l. 1-13; cf. ii. 29-30). These directions are very severe. The following actions are prohibited on the Sabbath under penalty of death: travelling by land or sea, buying or selling, drawing water, carrying burdens out of the house, killing or striking, snaring beasts, birds or fish, fasting or making war, marital intercourse. The last prescription is in direct opposition to Pharisaic practice, as is also the severe penalty imposed for non-observance of the various prescriptions. It is interesting to notice that these agree with the practice still maintained by the Falashas, Samaritans, and araite Jews. Probably this rigid view of sabbath-observance was cherished in specially pious priestly circles at the time when our author wrote. In this connexion it may be noted that our Book, in its interpretation of the law about the fruit of newly-planted trees given in Lev. xix. 23-24, agrees with the view of the Samaritans and araite Jews in directing that the first fruits of the fruit of the fourth year should be offered on the altar, and what remained given to the priests. According to Pharisaic practice what remained was to be eaten by the owners within the walls of Jerusalem.

Another point in which Jubilees upholds a view which is certainly not Pharisaic is on the question of the law of retribution, the so-called lex talionis. It is well known that while the Sadducees insisted on the strict letter of the Law, "an eye for an eye, and a tooth for a tooth," the Pharisees strove to mitigate its harshness by the substitution (except in the case of murder) of compensating money-payments. Moreover, the Mishna directs that where the death-penalty is inflicted it is to be carried out by the sword (cf. Sanhedrin ix. i: "These are to be beheaded"). Our Book, however, seems to wage a polemic against such views in no uncertain language: Take no gifts for the blood of man, lest it be shed with impunity, without judgement; for it is the blood that is shed that causes the earth to sin, and the earth cannot be cleansed from the blood of man save by the blood of him who shed it. And take no present or gift for the blood of man; blood for blood (xxi. 19 f.).

In iv. 31 f. the circumstances of Cain's death are described: his house fell upon him and he died in the midst of his house; for with a stone he had killed Abel, and by a stone was he killed in righteous judgement. For this reason it was ordained on the heavenly tables: "With the instrument with which a man kills his neighbour, with the same shall he be killed; after the manner that he wounded him, in like manner shall they deal with him."

It is true that a school of Pharisees (the School of Shammai) still, to some extent, upheld, in theory at any rate, the severer and older view. But this does not alter the fact that it was a distinctive tenet of the Sadducees; and it is difficult to believe that any Pharisee can, at any time, have used such unqualified language as that employed in the extracts given above.

At this point we may well ask what was the author's attitude towards the belief in a future life? At the time when he wrote the doctrine of the resurrection of the body had become well established in certain Jewish circles. In the Book of Daniel it had received classical expression. It was a cherished belief of the Pharisaic party. Now our Book does not in any way accept such a belief. The one passage in which the language employed might, at first sight, suggest a hint of such a belief is a sentence describing the happiness of the righteous in the age of felicity which is to dawn:

And at that time the Lord will heal His servants,
And they will rise up and see great peace,
And drive out their adversaries (xxiii. 30).

But here there is probably no reference to the idea of a resurrection. As Charles points out, the words "shall rise up" have here "apparently no reference to the resurrection, and mean merely that when God heals His servants (cf. Rev. xxii. 2) they become strong." The clause in the preceding verse, all their days will be days of blessing and healing (cf. also i. 29) renders "this view the most probable." On the other hand, the opening words of xxiii. 31

And their bones will rest in the earth,
And their spirits will have much joy,

though they are susceptible of another interpretation, may point to a belief that the righteous dead are destined to enjoy a blessed immortality. But it is to be noticed that no emphasis is laid on the idea; and in any case no countenance is given to the doctrine of resurrection. This attitude accords with the Sadducean position. What the Sadducees maintained was that the resurrection doctrine could not be proved from the Pentateuch. They did not assert that the personality was annihilated at death, or deny the doctrine of immortality--indeed, it is by no means impossible that some sections of the Sadducean party accepted this doctrine; but in general their position towards this question--apart from that of the bodily resurrection--was cautious and reserved. And this certainly seems to be the attitude of our author. It should be noted that Sheol is represented--somewhat vaguely and in poetical passages--as a place of punishment for the wicked (vii. 29; xxii. 22; xxiv. 31). This looks like the converse of the idea that the righteous dead are destined to enjoy a blessed immortality. In this connexion a word may be said about the angelology and demonology of our Book. These are in a fairly advanced stage, and imply much the same development as is to be seen in 1 Enoch and the Testaments of the XII Patriarchs. There are three classes of angels, two of a superior order, the angels of the presence, and the angels of sanctification (Cf. ii. 2, 18), and, besides these, a numerous inferior order who presided over natural phenomena (ii. 2). It is noteworthy that the two superior orders are represented as observing the

Sabbath, and as fulfilling the prescriptions of the Law regarding circumcision, etc.; they even observe in heaven the great festivals, such as the Feast of Weeks (vi. 18). 1 Various activities are assigned to the angels in connexion with mankind throughout our Book.

Over against the angelic orders there stands a well-organized demonic kingdom, presided over by "the prince of the Mastêmâ" (cf. xvii. 16; xlviii. 2; xviii. 9, 12, etc.). Among the Satanic beings that appear in our Book is Beliar (i. 20).

What is the attitude of our author towards the Messianic Hope? The hope for the coming of the Messianic King who should spring from the old Royal House of David was always cherished among the masses of the people, and in times of unusual stress was apt to flame up in vivid expression. The Pharisees, who themselves sprang from the ranks of the people, were naturally influenced by this tradition, and gave literary expression to it in the Psalms of Solomon (70-40 B.C.?). But at the time when our author wrote the desire for a Messianic King of the House of David was probably only latent. A period of national prosperity came in during the reign of John Hyrcanus, and the people generally were well content. It is not to be supposed, however, that the popular hope had completely died away. It was merely quiescent. On the other hand, there was a party, which no doubt had its seat in the priesthood, and may represent the old Saducean party, that claimed for the priesthood not only sacerdotal but also ruling functions: Levi's descendants are not only to be priests, but also the civil rulers of the nation, and this view receives expression in our Book (cf. xxxi. 15). Now it is well known that the Pharisees objected to the double office being exercised by one person, and when Alexander Jannæus assumed the title of "king" this feeling broke out into open hostility. At a somewhat later time a Pharisaic author in the Psalms of Solomon, looking back upon the terrible events that followed the breakup of the Hasmonean dynasty, evidently regards the bloody chastisement which the Jews had to endure at that time from the hands of the Romans as the punishment inflicted on the people for having acquiesced in the usurpation by the Hasmoneans of the royal dignity which had been reserved for the Messianic prince of the House of David. Especially significant in this connexion is the promise recounted in our Book of Levi (xxxii. i): And he abode that night at Bethel, and Levi dreamed that they had ordained and made him the Priest of the Most High God, him and his sons for ever. This, originally the title of the priest-king Melchizedek (Gen. xiv. 18), was revived by the Maccabean princely High Priests, and there is some evidence that in certain (? Saducean) quarters it was expected that the Messiah would spring from the tribe of Levi, and even from the priestly ruling Maccabean house. The one possible reference to the hope of a Messiah from Judah in our Book occurs in the blessing of Judah, xxxi. 18:

A prince shall thou be, thou and one of thy sons over the sons of Jacob;

Here Judah is addressed, and is singled out for special honour by the side of Levi. This was only natural, as the Jews derived their name from the tribe of Judah, who may be regarded as a sort of symbol of the nation generally. But who is meant by "one of thy sons"? Some would see in this a reference to the expected Messiah, but if this be so it is very vague. It is much more likely that the historic David is meant. The priestly author is significantly silent about a Davidic Messiah. Any Messiah he may have hoped for would, according to his view, spring from the tribe of Levi. He does not accept the view that the Davidic dynasty is of eternal duration, even ideally. May he not, too, have been thinking, in the address to Judah, of Judas Maccabæus? Judas by his warlike exploits had shed a new glory on the name "Judah." But Judas himself belonged to the priestly family of the Hasmoneans, and it would be easy for our author to see in him the embodiment of the glories of the tribe of Judah, without diminishing the claims of the priestly tribe to civil as well as sacerdotal primacy.

In the same context (xxxi. 20) two lines occur in the address to Judah which run as follows:

And when thou sittest on the throne of the honour of thy righteousness,
There will be great peace for all the seed of the sons of the beloved.

The exact meaning of these words is not clear. They can hardly refer to the expected Messiah from David's House, because in that case the context would demand the use of the third person, whereas the second person is employed and Judah is being addressed. Leszynsky suggests that here in the Hebrew original there may be an allusion to the Sadducees, suggested by a word-play in the Hebrew word for "righteousness" (sedek). But even so the sentence is not clear. Is our author still thinking of Judas Maccabæus? If so, he may mean "and when thou (Judas), in the person of thy High-Priestly successors, sittest as Priest-king on thy Sadducean throne of honour." It must be admitted that this is not very convincing, and the sentence remains obscure and uncertain in meaning. But of the high position assigned by our author to the tribe of Levi there can be no doubt. The lofty position of High-Priest and civil ruler is assigned to Levi as a reward for the destruction of Shechem (cf. xxx. 17-23; xxxii. 1-3). As Kohler says: "The Levites are represented as the keepers of the sacred books and of the secret lore entrusted to them by the saints from of yore (xlv. 16; cf. x. 14). This indicates that the priests and Levites still included among themselves, as in the days of the author of the Book of Chronicles, the men of learning, the masters of the schools, and that these positions were not filled by men from among the people, as was the case in the time of Shammai and Hillel." Other features of our Book entirely accord with this. For instance, the glorification of the Patriarchs in which our author loves to indulge is the development of a tendency already marked in the Priestly Sections of the Hexateuch. In Jubilees they become saints of the Law. Incidents which might reflect discredit upon them (such as that described in Gen. xii. 11-13) are omitted. Abram is represented as having known the true God from his youth (xi. 16-17; xii. i ff.). Jacob is "a model of filial affection and obedience." A noticeable feature is also the insistence upon the unique position of Israel among the nations, and its rigid separation from the latter. Circumcision is a sign of Israel's elect position (xv. 26) and a privilege which they enjoy in common with the two chief orders of angels (xv. 27). This is also true of the Sabbath, which the same angelic orders observe with Israel. It is needless to add that our author glorifies the Law, which is of heavenly origin and everlasting validity. This is his estimate of the Law in its narrow sense, i. e. the Pentateuch. It is by this criterion that he measures everything. It is true that Jubilees contains incidents and amplifications which are not to be found in the written Torah. But the author is careful to base everything that is of legal obligation upon the letter of the Law itself. Anything that he allows himself to introduce by way of amplification or addition serves merely to enhance the obligation of the written precept.

Finally, his eschatology is essentially that of one who is primarily interested in the Law. In xxiii. 12-31, he introduces an apocalyptic passage which gives a history of the Maccabean times from the persecution of Antiochus Epiphanes to the Messianic Kingdom, the advent of which is just at hand. A dark picture is drawn of the inroads of Hellenism, and of its disintegrating effects upon the observance of. the Law and the covenant (xxiii. 16-20); the warlike efforts of the Maccabees to reclaim the Hellenizers to Judaism are then described (xxiii. 20-22), and the cry of the nation for deliverance from its calamities (xxiii. 23-25). Then follows a passage (xxiii. 26-32) in which, as a consequence of Israel's renewed study of the Law, a happier period follows. The Messianic Kingdom is to be "brought about gradually by the progressive spiritual development of man and a corresponding transformation of nature." Its members are "to attain to the full limit of 1000 years in happiness and peace." Prof. Charles adds: "The writer of Jubilees, we can hardly doubt thought that the era of the Messianic Kingdom had already set in."

The important point to notice about this picture is that the dawn of the happier Age is brought about by renewed study and observance of the Law:

And in those days the children will begin to study the laws,
And to seek the commandments,
And to return to the Path of righteousness (xxiii. 26).

The result is a gradual transformation of men and their environment. There is no catastrophe. It is doubtful whether the author clearly envisages a final judgement, though there may be an allusion to such, in rather vague language, in xxiii. 30 f. The tone throughout is priestly, and it can hardly be doubted that the author was a priest.

Chapter 1

¹And it came to pass in the first year of the exodus of the children of Israel out of Egypt, in the third month, on the sixteenth day of the month, that God spake to Moses, saying: 'Come up to Me on the Mount, and I will give thee two tables of stone of the law and of the commandment, which ²I have written, that thou mayst teach them.' And Moses went up into the mount of God, and the ³glory of the Lord abode on Mount Sinai, and a cloud overshadowed it six days. And He called to Moses on the seventh day out of the midst of the cloud, and the appearance of the glory of the ⁴Lord was like a flaming fire on the top of the mount. And Moses was on the Mount forty days and forty nights, and God taught him the earlier and the later history of the division of all the days ⁵of the law and of the testimony. And He said: 'Incline thine heart to every word which I shall speak to thee on this mount, and write them in a book in order that their generations may see how I have not forsaken them for all the evil which they have wrought in transgressing the covenant ⁶which I establish between Me and thee for their generations this day on Mount Sinai. And thus it will come to pass when all these things come upon them, that they will recognise that I am more righteous than they in all their judgments and in all their actions, and they will recognise that ⁷I have been truly with them. And do thou write for thyself all these words which I declare unto, thee this day, for I know their rebellion and their stiff neck, before I bring them into the land of which I sware to their fathers, to Abraham and to Isaac and to Jacob, saying: ' Unto your seed ⁸will I give a land flowing with milk and honey. And they will eat and be satisfied, and they will turn to strange gods, to gods which cannot deliver them from aught of their tribulation: and this witness shall be heard for a witness against them. For they will forget all My commandments, even all that I command them, and they will walk after the Gentiles, and after their uncleanness, and after their shame, and will serve their gods, and these

will [10]prove unto them an offence and a tribulation and an affliction and a snare. And many will perish and they will be taken captive, and will fall into the hands of the enemy, because they have forsaken My ordinances and My commandments, and the festivals of My covenant, and My sabbaths, and My holy place which I have hallowed for Myself in their midst, and My tabernacle, and My sanctuary, which I have hallowed for Myself in the midst of the land, that I should set my name [11]upon it, and that it should dwell there. And they will make to themselves high places and groves and graven images, and they will worship, each his own graven image, so as to go astray, and they [12]will sacrifice their children to demons, and to all the works of the error of their hearts. And I will send witnesses unto them, that I may witness against them, but they will not hear, and will slay the witnesses also, and they will persecute those who seek the law, and they will abrogate and change [13]everything so as to work evil before My eyes. And I will hide My face from them, and I will deliver them into the hand of the Gentiles for captivity, and for a prey, and for devouring, and I will remove them from the midst of the land, and I will scatter them amongst the Gentiles. [14]And they will forget all My law and all My commandments and all My judgments, and will go [15]astray as to new moons, and sabbaths, and festivals, and jubilees, and ordinances. And after this they will turn to Me from amongst the Gentiles with all their heart and with all their soul and with all their strength, and I will gather them from amongst all the Gentiles, and they will seek me, so [16]that I shall be found of them, when they seek me with all their heart and with all their soul. And I will disclose to them abounding peace with righteousness, and I will remove them the plant of uprightness, with all My heart and with all My soul, and they shall be for a blessing and not for [17]a curse, and they shall be the head and not the tail. And I will build My sanctuary in their midst, and I will dwell with them, and I will be their God and they shall be My people in truth and [18], [19]righteousness. And I will not forsake them nor fail them; for I am the Lord their God.' And Moses fell on his face and prayed and said, 'O Lord my God, do not forsake Thy people and Thy inheritance, so that they should wander in the error of their hearts, and do not deliver them into the hands of their enemies, the Gentiles, lest they should rule over them and cause them to sin against [20]Thee. Let thy mercy, O Lord, be lifted up upon Thy people, and create in them an upright spirit, and let not the spirit of Beliar rule over them to accuse them before Thee, and to ensnare them [21]from all the paths of righteousness, so that they may perish from before Thy face. But they are Thy people and Thy inheritance, which thou hast delivered with thy great power from the hands of the Egyptians: create in them a clean heart and a holy spirit, and let them not be ensnared in [22]their sins from henceforth until eternity.' And the Lord said unto Moses: 'I know their contrariness and their thoughts and their stiffneckedness, and they will not be obedient till they confess [23]their own sin and the sin of their fathers. And after this they will turn to Me in all uprightness and with all their heart and with all their soul, and I will circumcise the foreskin of their heart and the foreskin of the heart of their seed, and I will create in them a holy spirit, and I will cleanse them so that they shall not turn away from Me from that day unto eternity. [24]And their souls will cleave to Me and to all My commandments, and they will fulfil My [25]commandments, and I will be their Father and they shall be My children. And they all shall be called children of the living God, and every angel and every spirit shall know, yea, they shall know that these are My children, and that I am their Father in uprightness and righteousness, and that [26]I love them. And do thou write down for thyself all these words which I declare unto thee on this mountain, the first and the last, which shall come to pass in all the divisions of the days in the law and in the testimony and in the weeks and the jubilees unto eternity, until I descend and dwell [27]with them throughout eternity.' And He said to the angel of the presence: Write for Moses from [28]the beginning of creation till My sanctuary has been built among them for all eternity. And the Lord will appear to the eyes of all, and all shall know that I am the God of Israel and the Father of all the children of Jacob, and King on Mount Zion for all eternity. And Zion and Jerusalem shall [29]be holy.' And the angel of the presence who went before the camp of Israel took the tables of the divisions of the years -from the time of the creation- of the law and of the testimony of the weeks of the jubilees, according to the individual years, according to all the number of the jubilees according, to the individual years, from the day of the new creation when the heavens and the earth shall be renewed and all their creation according to the powers of the heaven, and according to all the creation of the earth, until the sanctuary of the Lord shall be made in Jerusalem on Mount Zion, and all the luminaries be renewed for healing and for peace and for blessing for all the elect of Israel, and that thus it may be from that day and unto all the days of the earth.

Chapter 2

[1]And the angel of the presence spake to Moses according to the word of the Lord, saying: Write the complete history of the creation, how in six days the Lord God finished all His works and all that He created, and

kept Sabbath on the seventh day and hallowed it for all ages, and ²appointed it as a sign for all His works. For on the first day He created the heavens which are above and the earth and the waters and all the spirits which serve before him -the angels of the presence, and the angels of sanctification, and the angels of the spirit of fire and the angels of the spirit of the winds, and the angels of the spirit of the clouds, and of darkness, and of snow and of hail and of hoar frost, and the angels of the voices and of the thunder and of the lightning, and the angels of the spirits of cold and of heat, and of winter and of spring and of autumn and of summer and of all the spirits of his creatures which are in the heavens and on the earth, He created the abysses and the darkness, eventide and night, and the light, dawn and day, which He hath ³prepared in the knowledge of his heart. And thereupon we saw His works, and praised Him, and lauded before Him on account of all His works; for seven great works did He create on the first day. ⁴And on the second day He created the firmament in the midst of the waters, and the waters were divided on that day -half of them went up above and half of them went down below the firmament that was in the midst over the face of the whole earth. And this was the only work God created ⁵on the second day. And on the third day He commanded the waters to pass from off the face of ⁶the whole earth into one place, and the dry land to appear. And the waters did so as He commanded them, and they retired from off the face of the earth into one place outside of this firmament, ⁷and the dry land appeared. And on that day He created for them all the seas according to their separate gathering-places, and all the rivers, and the gatherings of the waters in the mountains and on all the earth, and all the lakes, and all the dew of the earth, and the seed which is sown, and all sprouting things, and fruit-bearing trees, and trees of the wood, and the garden of Eden, in Eden ⁸and all . These four great works God created on the third day. And on the fourth day He created the sun and the moon and the stars, and set them in the firmament of the heaven, to give light upon all the earth, and to rule over the day and the night, and divide the ⁹light from the darkness. And God appointed the sun to be a great sign on the earth for days and ¹⁰for sabbaths and for months and for feasts and for years and for sabbaths of years and for jubilees and for all seasons of the years. And it divideth the light from the darkness and for prosperity, that all things may prosper which shoot and grow on the earth. These three kinds He made on the fourth day. And on the fifth day He created great sea monsters in the depths of the waters, for these were the first things of flesh that were created by his hands, the fish and everything that moves in the

[12] waters, and everything that flies, the birds and all their kind. And the sun rose above them to prosper them, and above everything that was on the earth, everything that shoots out of the earth, and all [13] fruit-bearing trees, and all flesh. These three kinds He created on the fifth day. And on the sixth day [14] He created all the animals of the earth, and all cattle, and everything that moves on the earth. And after all this He created man, a man and a woman created He them, and gave him dominion over all that is upon the earth, and in the seas, and over everything that flies, and over beasts and over cattle, and over everything that moves on the earth, and over the whole earth, and over all this He gave [15] him dominion. And these four kinds He created on the sixth day. And there were altogether [16] two and twenty kinds. And He finished all his work on the sixth day -all that is in the heavens and on the earth, and in the seas and in the abysses, and in the light and in the darkness, and in [17] everything. And He gave us a great sign, the Sabbath day, that we should work six days, but [18] keep Sabbath on the seventh day from all work. And all the angels of the presence, and all the angels of sanctification, these two great classes -He hath bidden us to keep the Sabbath with Him [19] in heaven and on earth. And He said unto us: 'Behold, I will separate unto Myself a people from among all the peoples, and these shall keep the Sabbath day, and I will sanctify them unto Myself as My people, and will bless them; as I have sanctified the Sabbath day and do sanctify it unto [20] Myself, even so will I bless them, and they shall be My people and I will be their God. And I have chosen the seed of Jacob from amongst all that I have seen, and have written him down as My first-born son, and have sanctified him unto Myself for ever and ever; and I will teach them the [21] Sabbath day, that they may keep Sabbath thereon from all work.' And thus He created therein a sign in accordance with which they should keep Sabbath with us on the seventh day, to eat and to drink, and to bless Him who has created all things as He has blessed and sanctified unto Himself [22] a peculiar people above all peoples, and that they should keep Sabbath together with us. And He caused His commands to ascend as a sweet savour acceptable before Him all the days . . . [23] There were two and twenty heads of mankind from Adam to Jacob, and two and twenty kinds of work were made until the seventh day; this is blessed and holy; and the former also is blessed and [24] holy; and this one serves with that one for sanctification and blessing. And to this Jacob and his seed it was granted that they should always be the blessed and holy ones of the first testimony [25] and law, even as He had sanctified and blessed the Sabbath day on the seventh day. He created heaven and earth and

everything that He created in six days, and God made the seventh day holy, for all His works; therefore He commanded on its behalf that, whoever does any work thereon [26]shall die, and that he who defiles it shall surely die. Wherefore do thou command the children of Israel to observe this day that they may keep it holy and not do thereon any work, and not to [27]defile it, as it is holier than all other days. And whoever profanes it shall surely die, and whoever does thereon any work shall surely die eternally, that the children of Israel may observe this day throughout their generations, and not be rooted out of the land; for it is a holy day and a blessed [28]day. And every one who observes it and keeps Sabbath thereon from all his work, will be holy and [29]blessed throughout all days like unto us. Declare and say to the children of Israel the law of this day both that they should keep Sabbath thereon, and that they should not forsake it in the error of their hearts; and that it is not lawful to do any work thereon which is unseemly, to do thereon their own pleasure, and that they should not prepare thereon anything to be eaten or drunk, and that it is not lawful to draw water, or bring in or take out thereon through their gates any burden, [30]which they had not prepared for themselves on the sixth day in their dwellings. And they shall not bring in nor take out from house to house on that day; for that day is more holy and blessed than any jubilee day of the jubilees; on this we kept Sabbath in the heavens before it was made [31]known to any flesh to keep Sabbath thereon on the earth. And the Creator of all things blessed it, but he did not sanctify all peoples and nations to keep Sabbath thereon, but Israel alone: them [32]alone he permitted to eat and drink and to keep Sabbath thereon on the earth. And the Creator of all things blessed this day which He had created for blessing and holiness and glory above all [33]days. This law and testimony was given to the children of Israel as a law for ever unto their generations.

Chapter 3

[1]And on the six days of the second week we brought, according to the word of God, unto Adam all the beasts, and all the cattle, and all the birds, and everything that moves on the earth, and everything that moves in the water, according to their kinds, and according to their types: the beasts on the first day; the cattle on the second day; the birds on the third day; and all that which moves on the earth on the fourth day; and that which moves in the water on the fifth day. [2]And Adam named them all by their respective names, and as he called them, so was their name. [3]And on these five days Adam saw all these, male and female, according to every kind that was on [4]the earth, but he was alone and found no helpmeet for him.

And the Lord said unto us: 'It is not ⁵good that the man should be alone: let us make a helpmeet for him.' And the Lord our God caused a deep sleep to fall upon him, and he slept, and He took for the woman one rib from amongst ⁶his ribs, and this rib was the origin of the woman from amongst his ribs, and He built up the flesh in its stead, and built the woman. And He awaked Adam out of his sleep and on awaking he rose on the sixth day, and He brought her to him, and he knew her, and said unto her: 'This is now bone of my bones and flesh of my flesh; she shall be called ⁷my wife; because she was taken from her husband.' Therefore shall man and wife be one and therefore shall a man leave his father and his mother, and cleave unto his wife, and they shall be ⁸one flesh. In the first week was Adam created, and the rib -his wife: in the second week He showed her unto him: and for this reason the commandment was given to keep in their defilement, ⁹for a male seven days, and for a female twice seven days. And after Adam had completed forty days in the land where he had been created, we brought him into the garden of Eden to till and keep it, but his wife they brought in on the eightieth day, and after this she entered into the garden ¹⁰of Eden. And for this reason the commandment is written on the heavenly tablets in regard to her that gives birth: 'if she bears a male, she shall remain in her uncleanness seven days according to the first week of days, and thirty and three days shall she remain in the blood of her purifying, and she shall not touch any hallowed thing, nor enter into the sanctuary, until she accomplishes these ¹¹days which are enjoined in the case of a male child. But in the case of a female child she shall remain in her uncleanness two weeks of days, according to the first two weeks, and sixty-six days ¹²in the blood of her purification, and they will be in all eighty days.' And when she had completed these eighty days we brought her into the garden of Eden, for it is holier than all the earth besides and ¹³every tree that is planted in it is holy. Therefore, there was ordained regarding her who bears a male or a female child the statute of those days that she should touch no hallowed thing, nor ¹⁴enter into the sanctuary until these days for the male or female child are accomplished. This is the law and testimony which was written down for Israel, in order that they should observe it all the ¹⁵days. And in the first week of the first jubilee, Adam and his wife were in the garden of Eden for seven years tilling and keeping it, and we gave him work and we instructed him to do everything ¹⁶that is suitable for tillage. And he tilled the garden, and was naked and knew it not, and was not ashamed, and he protected the garden from the birds and beasts and cattle, and gathered its fruit, and eat, and put aside the residue for himself and for his wife and put aside that which was [17]being kept. And after the completion of the seven years, which he had completed there, seven years exactly, and in the second month, on the seventeenth day of the month, the serpent came and approached the woman, and the serpent said to the woman, 'Hath God commanded you, [18]saying, Ye shall not eat of every tree of the garden' And she said to it, 'Of all the fruit of the trees of the garden God hath said unto us, Eat; but of the fruit of the tree which is in the midst of the garden God hath said unto us, Ye shall not eat thereof, neither shall ye touch it, lest ye die.' And the serpent said unto the woman, 'Ye shall not surely die: for God doth know that on the day ye shall eat thereof, your eyes will be opened, and ye will be as gods, and ye will know good and [20]evil. And the woman saw the tree that it was agreeable and pleasant to the eye, and that its fruit [21]was good for food, and she took thereof and eat. And when she had first covered her shame with figleaves, she gave thereof to Adam and he eat, and his eyes were opened, and he saw that he was [22]naked. And he took figleaves and sewed them together, and made an apron for himself, and [23], [24]covered his shame. And God cursed the serpent, and was wroth with it for ever . . . And He was wroth with the woman, because she harkened to the voice of the serpent, and did eat; and He said unto her: 'I will greatly multiply thy sorrow and thy pains: in sorrow thou shalt bring forth [25]children, and thy return shall be unto thy husband, and he will rule over thee.' And to Adam also he said, ' Because thou hast harkened unto the voice of thy wife, and hast eaten of the tree of which I commanded thee that thou shouldst not eat thereof, cursed be the ground for thy sake: thorns and thistles shall it bring forth to thee, and thou shalt eat thy bread in the sweat of thy face, till thou returnest to the earth from whence thou wast taken; for earth thou art, and unto earth shalt [26]thou return.' And He made for them coats of skin, and clothed them, and sent them forth from [27]the Garden of Eden. And on that day on which Adam went forth from the Garden, he offered as a sweet savour an offering, frankincense, galbanum, and stacte, and spices in the morning with the [28]rising of the sun from the day when he covered his shame. And on that day was closed the mouth of all beasts, and of cattle, and of birds, and of whatever walks, and of whatever moves, so that they could no longer speak: for they had all spoken one with another with one lip and with one tongue. [29]And He sent out of the Garden of Eden all flesh that was in the Garden of Eden, and all flesh was scattered according to its kinds, and according to its types unto the places which had been created [30]for them. And to Adam alone did He give the wherewithal to cover his shame, of all the beasts and ³¹cattle. On this account, it is prescribed on the heavenly tablets as touching all those who know the judgment of the law, that they should cover their shame, and should not uncover themselves as the ³²Gentiles uncover themselves. And on the new moon of the fourth month, Adam and his wife went ³³forth from the Garden of Eden, and they dwelt in the land of Elda in the land of their creation. And ³⁴Adam called the name of his wife Eve. And they had no son till the first jubilee, and after this he ³⁵knew her. Now he tilled the land as he had been instructed in the Garden of Eden.

Chapter 4

¹And in the third week in the second jubilee she gave birth to Cain, and in the fourth she gave birth to Abel, and in the fifth she gave birth to her daughter Awan. And in the first year of the third jubilee, Cain slew Abel because God accepted the sacrifice of Abel, and did not accept ³the offering of Cain. And he slew him in the field: and his blood cried from the ground to heaven, ⁴complaining because he had slain him. And the Lord reproved Cain because of Abel, because he had slain him, and he made him a fugitive on the earth because of the blood of his brother, and he ⁵cursed him upon the earth. And on this account it is written on the heavenly tables, 'Cursed is ,he who smites his neighbour treacherously, and let all who have seen and heard say, So be it; and ⁶the man who has seen and not declared it, let him be accursed as the other.' And for this reason we announce when we come before the Lord our God all the sin which is committed in heaven and ⁷on earth, and in light and in darkness, and everywhere. And Adam and his wife mourned for Abel four weeks of years, and in the fourth year of the fifth week they became joyful, and Adam knew his wife again, and she bare him a son, and he called his name Seth; for he said 'GOD has ⁸raised up a second seed unto us on the earth instead of Abel; for Cain slew him.' And in the sixth ⁹week he begat his daughter Azura. And Cain took Awan his sister to be his wife and she bare him Enoch at the close of the fourth jubilee. And in the first year of the first week of the fifth jubilee, houses were built on the earth, and Cain built a city, and called its name after the name of ¹⁰, ¹¹his son Enoch. And Adam knew Eve his wife and she bare yet nine sons. And in the fifth week of the fifth jubilee Seth took Azura his sister to be his wife, and in the fourth year of the sixth ¹²,¹³week she bare him Enos. He began to call on the name of the Lord on the earth. And in the seventh jubilee in the third week Enos took Noam his sister to be his wife, and she bare him a son ¹⁴in the third year of the fifth week, and he called his name Kenan. And at the close of the eighth jubilee Kenan took

Mualeleth his sister to be his wife, and she bare him a son in the ninth jubilee, [15]in the first week in the third year of this week, and he called his name Mahalalel. And in the second week of the tenth jubilee Mahalalel took unto him to wife DinaH, the daughter of Barakiel the daughter of his father's brother, and she bare him a son in the third week in the sixth year, and he called his name Jared, for in his days the angels of the Lord descended on the earth, those who are named the Watchers, that they should instruct the children of men, and that they should do [16]judgment and uprightness on the earth. And in the eleventh jubilee Jared took to himself a wife, and her name was Baraka, the daughter of Rasujal, a daughter of his father's brother, in the fourth week of this jubilee, and she bare him a son in the fifth week, in the fourth year of the jubilee, and [17]he called his name Enoch. And he was the first among men that are born on earth who learnt writing and knowledge and wisdom and who wrote down the signs of heaven according to the order of their months in a book, that men might know the seasons of the years according to the order of [18]their separate months. And he was the first to write a testimony and he testified to the sons of men among the generations of the earth, and recounted the weeks of the jubilees, and made known to them the days of the years, and set in order the months and recounted the Sabbaths of the years [19]as we made them, known to him. And what was and what will be he saw in a vision of his sleep, as it will happen to the children of men throughout their generations until the day of judgment; he saw and understood everything, and wrote his testimony, and placed the testimony on earth for all [20]the children of men and for their generations. And in the twelfth jubilee, in the seventh week thereof, he took to himself a wife, and her name was Edna, the daughter of Danel, the daughter of his father's brother, and in the sixth year in this week she bare him a son and he called his name [21]Methuselah. And he was moreover with the angels of God these six jubilees of years, and they showed him everything which is on earth and in the heavens, the rule of the sun, and he wrote down [22]everything. And he testified to the Watchers, who had sinned with the daughters of men; for these had begun to unite themselves, so as to be defiled, with the daughters of men, and Enoch [23]testified against them all. And he was taken from amongst the children of men, and we conducted him into the Garden of Eden in majesty and honour, and behold there he writes down the con-[24]demnation and judgment of the world, and all the wickedness of the children of men. And on account of it God brought the waters of the flood upon all the land of Eden; for there he was set as a sign and that he should testify against all the children of men, that he should recount all the [25]deeds of the generations until the day of condemnation. And he burnt the incense of the sanctuary, [26]even sweet spices acceptable before the Lord on the Mount. For the Lord has four places on the earth, the Garden of Eden, and the Mount of the East, and this mountain on which thou art this day, Mount Sinai, and Mount Zion which will be sanctified in the new creation for a sanctification of the earth; through it will the earth be sanctified from all its guilt and its uncleanness through- [27]out the generations of the world. And in the fourteenth jubilee Methuselah took unto himself a wife, Edna the daughter of Azrial, the daughter of his father's brother, in the third week, in the [28]first year of this week, and he begat a son and called his name Lamech. And in the fifteenth jubilee in the third week Lamech took to himself a wife, and her name was Betenos the daughter of Baraki'il, the daughter of his father's brother, and in this week she bare him a son and he called his name Noah, saying, 'This one will comfort me for my trouble and all my work, and for the ground [29]which the Lord hath cursed.' And at the close of the nineteenth jubilee, in the seventh week in the sixth year thereof, Adam died, and all his sons buried him in the land of his creation, and he [30]was the first to be buried in the earth. And he lacked seventy years of one thousand years; for one thousand years are as one day in the testimony of the heavens and therefore was it written concerning the tree of knowledge: 'On the day that ye eat thereof ye shall die.' For this reason he [31]did not complete the years of this day; for he died during it. At the close of this jubilee Cain was killed after him in the same year; for his house fell upon him and he died in the midst of his house, and he was killed by its stones; for with a stone he had killed Abel, and by a stone was he killed in [32]righteous judgment. For this reason it was ordained on the heavenly tablets: With the instrument with which a man kills his neighbour with the same shall he be killed; after the manner that [33]he wounded him, in like manner shall they deal with him.' And in the twenty-fifth jubilee Noah took to himself a wife, and her name was Emzara, the daughter of Rake'el, the daughter of his father's brother, in the first year in the fifth week: and in the third year thereof she bare him Shem, in the fifth year thereof she bare him Ham, and in the first year in the sixth week she bare him Japheth.

Chapter 5

[1]And it came to pass when the children of men began to multiply on the face of the earth and daughters were born unto them, that the angels of God saw them on a certain year of this jubilee, that they were beautiful to look upon; and they took themselves

wives of all whom they [2]chose, and they bare unto them sons and they were giants. And lawlessness increased on the earth and all flesh corrupted its way, alike men and cattle and beasts and birds and everything that walks on the earth -all of them corrupted their ways and their orders, and they began to devour each other, and lawlessness increased on the earth and every imagination of the thoughts of all men [3]was thus evil continually. And God looked upon the earth, and behold it was corrupt, and all flesh had corrupted its orders, and all that were upon the earth had wrought all manner of evil [4]before His eyes. And He said that He would destroy man and all flesh upon the face of the earth [5],[6]which He had created. But Noah found grace before the eyes of the Lord. And against the angels whom He had sent upon the earth, He was exceedingly wroth, and He gave commandment to root them out of all their dominion, and He bade us to bind them in the depths of the earth, and [7]behold they are bound in the midst of them, and are kept separate. And against their sons went forth a command from before His face that they should be smitten with the sword, and be removed [8]from under heaven. And He said 'My spirit shall not always abide on man; for they also are flesh [9]and their days shall be one hundred and twenty years'. And He sent His sword into their midst that each should slay his neighbour, and they began to slay each other till they all fell by the sword [10]and were destroyed from the earth. And their fathers were witnesses of their destruction, and after this they were bound in the depths of the earth for ever, until the day of the great condemnation, when judgment is executed on all those who have corrupted their ways and their works before [11]the Lord. And He destroyed all from their places, and there was not left one of them whom [12]He judged not according to all their wickedness. And he made for all his works a new and righteous nature, so that they should not sin in their whole nature for ever, but should be all [13]righteous each in his kind alway. And the judgment of all is ordained and written on the heavenly tablets in righteousness -even the judgment of all who depart from the path which is ordained for them to walk in; and if they walk not therein, judgment is written down for every creature and [14]for every kind. And there is nothing in heaven or on earth, or in light or in darkness, or in Sheol or in the depth, or in the place of darkness which is not judged; and all their judgments are [15]ordained and written and engraved. In regard to all He will judge,the great according to his [16]greatness, and the small according to his smallness, and each according to his way. And He is not one who will regard the person of any, nor is He one who will receive gifts, if He says that He will execute judgment on each: if one gave everything that is on the earth, He will not regard the [17]gifts or the person of any, nor accept anything at his hands, for He is a righteous judge. And of the children of Israel it has been written and ordained: If they turn to him in righteousness He will forgive all their transgressions and pardon all their sins. It is written and ordained that [19]He will show mercy to all who turn from all their guilt once each year. And as for all those who corrupted their ways and their thoughts before the flood, no man's person was accepted save that of Noah alone; for his person was accepted in behalf of his sons, whom God saved from the waters of the flood on his account; for his heart was righteous in all his ways, according as it was com- [20]manded regarding him, and he had not departed from aught that was ordained for him. And the Lord said that he would destroy everything which was upon the earth, both men and cattle, and [21]beasts, and fowls of the air, and that which moveth on the earth. And He commanded Noah to [22]make him an ark, that he might save himself from the waters of the flood. And Noah made the ark in all respects as He commanded him, in the twenty-seventh jubilee of years, in the fifth week [23]in the fifth year on the new moon of the first month. And he entered in the sixth year thereof, in the second month, on the new moon of the second month, till the sixteenth; and he entered, and all that we brought to him, into the ark, and the Lord closed it from without on the seventeenth evening. [24]And the Lord opened seven flood-gates of heaven, And the mouths of the fountains of the great deep, seven mouths in number. [25]And the flood-gates began to pour down water from the heaven forty days and forty nights, And the fountains of the deep also sent up waters, until the whole world was full of water. [26]And the waters increased upon the earth: Fifteen cubits did the waters rise above all the high mountains, And the ark was lift up above the earth, And it moved upon the face of the waters. [27]And the water prevailed on the face of the earth five months -one hundred and fifty days. [28], [29]And the ark went and rested on the top of Lubar, one of the mountains of Ararat. And on the new moon in the fourth month the fountains of the great deep were closed and the flood-gates of heaven were restrained; and on the new moon of the seventh month all the mouths of the abysses [30]of the earth were opened, and the water began to descend into the deep below. And on the new moon of the tenth month the tops of the mountains were seen, and on the new moon of the first [31]month the earth became visible. And the waters disappeared from above the earth in the fifth week in the seventh year thereof, and on the seventeenth day in the second month the earth was dry. [32]And on the twenty-seventh thereof he opened the ark, and sent forth from it beasts, and cattle, and birds, and every moving thing.

Chapter 6

[1]And on the new moon of the third month he went forth from the ark, and built an altar on [2]that mountain. And he made atonement for the earth, and took a kid and made atonement by its blood for all the guilt of the earth; for everything that had been on it had been destroyed, save [3]those that were in the ark with Noah. And he placed the fat thereof on the altar, and he took an ox, and a goat, and a sheep and kids, and salt, and a turtle-dove, and the young of a dove, and placed a burnt sacrifice on the altar, and poured thereon an offering mingled with oil, and sprinkled wine and strewed frankincense over everything, and caused a goodly savour to arise, acceptable before [4]the Lord. And the Lord smelt the goodly savour, and He made a covenant with him that there should not be any more a flood to destroy the earth; that all the days of the earth seed-time and harvest should never cease; cold and heat, and summer and winter, and day and night should not [5]change their order, nor cease for ever. 'And you, increase ye and multiply upon the earth, and become many upon it, and be a blessing upon it. The fear of you and the dread of you I will [6]inspire in everything that is on earth and in the sea. And behold I have given unto you all beasts, and all winged things, and everything that moves on the earth, and the fish in the waters, and all [7]things for food; as the green herbs, I have given you all things to eat. But flesh, with the life thereof, with the blood, ye shall not eat; for the life of all flesh is in the blood, lest your blood of your lives be required. At the hand of every man, at the hand of every beast will I require the [8]blood of man. Whoso sheddeth man's blood by man shall his blood be shed, for in the image of [9],[10]God made He man. And you, increase ye, and multiply on the earth.' And Noah and his sons swore that they would not eat any blood that was in any flesh, and he made a covenant before the [11]Lord God for ever throughout all the generations of the earth in this month. On this account He spake to thee that thou shouldst make a covenant with the children of Israel in this month upon the mountain with an oath, and that thou shouldst sprinkle blood upon them because of all the words [12]of the covenant, which the Lord made with them for ever. And this testimony is written concerning you that you should observe it continually, so that you should not eat on any day any blood of beasts or birds or cattle during all the days of the earth, and the man who eats the blood of beast or of cattle or of birds during all the days of the earth, he and his seed shall be rooted out of the land. [13]And do thou command the children of Israel to eat

no blood, so that their names and their seed [14]may be before the Lord our God continually. And for this law there is no limit of days, for it is for ever. They shall observe it throughout their generations, so that they may continue supplicating on your behalf with blood before the altar; every day and at the time of morning and evening they shall seek forgiveness on your behalf perpetually before the Lord that they may keep [15]it and not be rooted out. And He gave to Noah and his sons a sign that there should not again [16]be a flood on the earth. He set His bow in the cloud for a sign of the eternal covenant that there [17]should not again be a flood on the earth to destroy it all the days of the earth. For this reason it is ordained and written on the heavenly tablets, that they should celebrate the feast of weeks in this [18]month once a year, to renew the covenant every year. And this whole festival was celebrated in heaven from the day of creation till the days of Noah -twenty-six jubilees and five weeks of years: and Noah and his sons observed it for seven jubilees and one week of years, till the day of Noah's death, and from the day of Noah's death his sons did away with it until the days of Abraham, and [19]they eat blood. But Abraham observed it, and Isaac and Jacob and his children observed it up to thy days, and in thy days the children of Israel forgot it until ye celebrated it anew on this mountain. [20]And do thou command the children of Israel to observe this festival in all their generations for a [21]commandment unto them: one day in the year in this month they shall celebrate the festival. For it is the feast of weeks and the feast of first fruits: this feast is twofold and of a double nature: [22]according to what is written and engraven concerning it, celebrate it. For I have written in the book of the first law, in that which I have written for thee, that thou shouldst celebrate it in its season, one day in the year, and I explained to thee its sacrifices that the children of Israel should remember and should celebrate it throughout their generations in this month, one day in every year. [23]And on the new moon of the first month, and on the new moon of the fourth month, and on the new moon of the seventh month, and on the new moon of the tenth month are the days of remembrance, and the days of the seasons in the four divisions of the year. These are written and ordained [24]as a testimony for ever. And Noah ordained them for himself as feasts for the generations for ever, [25]so that they have become thereby a memorial unto him. And on the new moon of the first month he was bidden to make for himself an ark, and on that day the earth became dry and he opened [26]the ark and saw the earth. And on the new moon of the fourth month the mouths of the depths of the abyss beneath were closed. And on the new moon of the seventh month all the mouths of

[27] the abysses of the earth were opened, and the waters began to descend into them. And on the new [28] moon of the tenth month the tops of the mountains were seen, and Noah was glad. And on this account he ordained them for himself as feasts for a memorial for ever, and thus are they ordained. [29] And they placed them on the heavenly tablets, each had thirteen weeks; from one to another passed their memorial, from the first to the second, and from the second to the third, and from the [30] third to the fourth. And all the days of the commandment will be two and fifty weeks of days, and these will make the entire year complete. Thus it is engraven and ordained on the heavenly [31] tablets. And there is no neglecting this commandment for a single year or from year to year. [32] And command thou the children of Israel that they observe the years according to this reckoning- three hundred and sixty-four days, and these will constitute a complete year, and they will not disturb its time from its days and from its feasts; for everything will fall out in them according to [33] their testimony, and they will not leave out any day nor disturb any feasts. But if they do neglect and do not observe them according to His commandment, then they will disturb all their seasons and the years will be dislodged from this order, and they will disturb the seasons and the years [34] will be dislodged and they will neglect their ordinances. And all the children of Israel will forget and will not find the path of the years, and will forget the new moons, and seasons, and sabbaths [35] and they will go wrong as to all the order of the years. For I know and from henceforth will I declare it unto thee, and it is not of my own devising; for the book lies written before me, and on the heavenly tablets the division of days is ordained, lest they forget the feasts of the covenant [36] and walk according to the feasts of the Gentiles after their error and after their ignorance. For there will be those who will assuredly make observations of the moon -how it disturbs the [37] seasons and comes in from year to year ten days too soon. For this reason the years will come upon them when they will disturb the order, and make an abominable day the day of testimony, and an unclean day a feast day, and they will confound all the days, the holy with the unclean, and the unclean day with the holy; for they will go wrong as to the months and sabbaths and feasts and [38] jubilees. For this reason I command and testify to thee that thou mayst testify to them; for after thy death thy children will disturb them, so that they will not make the year three hundred and sixty-four days only, and for this reason they will go wrong as to the new moons and seasons and sabbaths and festivals, and they will eat all kinds of blood with all kinds of flesh.

Chapter 7

¹And in the seventh week in the first year thereof, in this jubilee, Noah planted vines on the mountain on which the ark had rested, named Lubar, one of the Ararat Mountains, and they produced fruit in the fourth year, and he guarded their fruit, and gathered it in this year in the ²seventh month. And he made wine therefrom and put it into a vessel, and kept it until the fifth ³year, until the first day, on the new moon of the first month. And he celebrated with joy the day of this feast, and he made a burnt sacrifice unto the Lord, one young ox and one ram, and seven sheep, each a year old, and a kid of the goats, that he might make atonement thereby for himself ⁴and his sons. And he prepared the kid first, and placed some of its blood on the flesh that was on the altar which he had made, and all the fat he laid on the altar where he made the burnt sacrifice, ⁵and the ox and the ram and the sheep, and he laid all their flesh upon the altar. And he placed all their offerings mingled with oil upon it, and afterwards he sprinkled wine on the fire which he had previously made on the altar, and he placed incense on the altar and caused a sweet savour to ⁶ascend acceptable before the Lord his God. And he rejoiced and drank of this wine, he and his ⁷children with joy. And it was evening, and he went into his tent, and being drunken he lay down ⁸and slept, and was uncovered in his tent as he slept. And Ham saw Noah his father naked, and ⁹went forth and told his two brethren without. And Shem took his garment and arose, he and Japheth, and they placed the garment on their shoulders and went backward and covered the shame ¹⁰of their father, and their faces were backward. And Noah awoke from his sleep and knew all that his younger son had done unto him, and he cursed his son and said: 'Cursed be Canaan; an ¹¹enslaved servant shall he be unto his brethren.' And he blessed Shem, and said: 'Blessed be the ¹²Lord God of Shem, and Canaan shall be his servant. God shall enlarge Japheth, and God shall ¹³dwell in the dwelling of Shem, and Canaan shall be his servant.' And Ham knew that his father had cursed his younger son, and he was displeased that he had cursed his son. and he parted from ¹⁴his father, he and his sons with him, Cush and Mizraim and Put and Canaan. And he built for ¹⁵himself a city and called its name after the name of his wife Ne'elatama'uk. And Japheth saw it, and became envious of his brother, and he too built for himself a city, and he called its name after ¹⁶the name of his wife 'Adataneses. And Shem dwelt with his father Noah, and he built a city close to his father on the mountain, and he too called its name after the name of his wife Sedeqetelebab. ¹⁷And behold these three cities are near Mount Lubar; Sedeqetelebab fronting the mountain

on its [18]east; and Na'eltama'uk on the south; 'Adatan'eses towards the west. And these are the sons of Shem: Elam, and Asshur, and Arpachshad -this son was born two years after the flood- and [19]Lud, and Aram. The sons of Japheth: Gomer and Magog and Madai and Javan, Tubal and [20]Meshech and Tiras: these are the sons of Noah. And in the twenty-eighth jubilee Noah began to enjoin upon his sons' sons the ordinances and commandments, and all the judgments that he knew, and he exhorted his sons to observe righteousness, and to cover the shame of their flesh, and to bless their Creator, and honour father and mother, and love their neighbour, and guard their souls [21]from fornication and uncleanness and all iniquity. For owing to these three things came the flood upon the earth, namely, owing to the fornication wherein the Watchers against the law of their ordinances went a whoring after the daughters of men, and took themselves wives of all which they [22]chose: and they made the beginning of uncleanness. And they begat sons the Naphidim, and they were all unlike, and they devoured one another: and the Giants slew the Naphil, and the [23]Naphil slew the Eljo, and the Eljo mankind, and one man another. And every one sold himself [24]to work iniquity and to shed much blood, and the earth was filled with iniquity. And after this they sinned against the beasts and birds, and all that moves and walks on the earth: and much blood was shed on the earth, and every imagination and desire of men imagined vanity and evil [25]continually. And the Lord destroyed everything from off the face of the earth; because of the wickedness of their deeds, and because of the blood which they had shed in the midst of the earth [26]He destroyed everything. 'And we were left, I and you, my sons, and everything that entered with us into the ark, and behold I see your works before me that ye do not walk in righteousness: for in the path of destruction ye have begun to walk, and ye are parting one from another, and are envious one of another, and so it comes that ye are not in harmony, my sons, each with his brother. [27]For I see, and behold the demons have begun their seductions against you and against your children and now I fear on your behalf, that after my death ye will shed the blood of men upon the earth, [28]and that ye, too, will be destroyed from the face of the earth. For whoso sheddeth man's blood, and whoso eateth the blood of any flesh, shall all be destroyed from the earth. [29]And there shall not be left any man that eateth blood, or that sheddeth the blood of man on the earth, Nor shall there be left to him any seed or descendants living under heaven; For into Sheol shall they go, And into the place of condemnation shall they descend, And into the darkness of the deep shall they all be removed by a violent death. ³⁰There shall be no blood seen upon you of all the blood there shall be all the days in which ye have killed any beasts or cattle or whatever flies upon the earth, and work ye a good work to your ³¹souls by covering that which has been shed on the face of the earth. And ye shall not be like him who eats with blood, but guard yourselves that none may eat blood before you: cover the blood, ³²for thus have I been commanded to testify to you and your children, together with all flesh. And suffer not the soul to be eaten with the flesh, that your blood, which is your life, may not be required ³³at the hand of any flesh that sheds it on the earth. For the earth will not be clean from the blood which has been shed upon it; for only through the blood of him that shed it will the earth be ³⁴purified throughout all its generations. And now, my children, harken: work judgment and righteousness that ye maybe planted in righteousness over the face of the whole earth, and your ³⁵glory lifted up before my God, who saved me from the waters of the flood. And behold, ye will go and build for yourselves cities, and plant in them all the plants that are upon the earth, and moreover ³⁶all fruit-bearing trees. For three years the fruit of everything that is eaten will not be gathered: and in the fourth year its fruit will be accounted holy and they will offer the first-fruits, acceptable before the Most High God, who created heaven and earth and all things. Let them offer in abundance the first of the wine and oil as first-fruits on the altar of the Lord, who receives it, and ³⁷what is left let the servants of the house of the Lord eat before the altar which receives it. And in the fifth year make ye the release so that ye release it in righteousness and uprightness, and ye shall be righteous, ³⁸and all that you plant shall prosper. For thus did Enoch, the father of your father command Methuselah, his son, and Methuselah his son Lamech, and Lamech commanded me all the things ³⁹which his fathers commanded him. And I also will give you commandment, my sons, as Enoch commanded his son in the first jubilees: whilst still living, the seventh in his generation, he commanded and testified to his son and to his son's sons until the day of his death.'

Chapter 8

¹In the twenty-ninth jubilee, in the first week, in the beginning thereof Arpachshad took to himself a wife and her name was Rasu'eja, the daughter of Susan, the daughter of Elam, and she ²bare him a son in the third year in this week, and he called his name Kainam. And the son grew, and his father taught him writing, and he went to seek for himself a place where he might seize for ³himself a city. And he found a writing which former generations had carved on the rock, and he read what was thereon, and he

transcribed it and sinned owing to it; for it contained the teaching of the Watchers in accordance with which they used to observe the omens of the sun and moon and [4]stars in all the signs of heaven. And he wrote it down and said nothing regarding it; for he was [5]afraid to speak to Noah about it lest he should be angry with him on account of it. And in the thirtieth jubilee, in the second week, in the first year thereof, he took to himself a wife, and her name was Melka, the daughter of Madai, the son of Japheth, and in the fourth year he begat a son, and [6]called his name Shelah; for he said: 'Truly I have been sent.' And in the fourth year he was born, and Shelah grew up and took to himself a wife, and her name was Mu'ak, the daughter of Kesed, his father's brother, in the one and thirtieth jubilee, in the fifth week, in the first year [7]thereof. And she bare him a son in the fifth year thereof, and he called his name Eber: and he took unto himself a wife, and her name was 'Azurad, the daughter of Nebrod, in the thirty-second [8]jubilee, in the seventh week, in the third year thereof. And in the sixth year thereof, she bare him son, and he called his name Peleg; for in the days when he was born the children of Noah began [9]to divide the earth amongst themselves: for this reason he called his name Peleg. And they [10]divided it secretly amongst themselves, and told it to Noah. And it came to pass in the beginning of the thirty-third jubilee that they divided the earth into three parts, for Shem and Ham and Japheth, according to the inheritance of each, in the first year in the first week, when one of us [11]who had been sent, was with them. And he called his sons, and they drew nigh to him, they and their children, and he divided the earth into the lots, which his three sons were to take in possession, and they reached forth their hands, and took the writing out of the bosom of Noah, their father. [12]And there came forth on the writing as Shem's lot the middle of the earth which he should take as an inheritance for himself and for his sons for the generations of eternity, from the middle of the mountain range of Rafa, from the mouth of the water from the river Tina, and his portion goes towards the west through the midst of this river, and it extends till it reaches the water of the abysses, out of which this river goes forth and pours its waters into the sea Me'at, and this river flows into the great sea. And all that is towards the north is Japheth's, and all that is towards the [13]south belongs to Shem. And it extends till it reaches Karaso: this is in the bosom of the tongue [14]which looks towards the south. And his portion extends along the great sea, and it extends in a straight line till it reaches the west of the tongue which looks towards the south: for this sea is [15]named the tongue of the Egyptian Sea. And it turns from here towards the south towards the mouth of the great sea on the shore of its waters, and it extends to the west to 'Afra, and it extends till it reaches the waters of the river Gihon, and to the south of the waters of Gihon, to the [16]banks of this river. And it extends towards the east, till it reaches the Garden of Eden, to the south thereof, to the south and from the east of the whole land of Eden and of the whole east, it turns to the east and proceeds till it reaches the east of the mountain named Rafa, and it descends [17]to the bank of the mouth of the river Tina. This portion came forth by lot for Shem and his sons, [18]that they should possess it for ever unto his generations for evermore. And Noah rejoiced that this portion came forth for Shem and for his sons, and he remembered all that he had spoken with his mouth in prophecy; for he had said: 'Blessed be the Lord God of Shem And may the Lord dwell in the dwelling of Shem.' [19]And he knew that the Garden of Eden is the holy of holies, and the dwelling of the Lord, and Mount Sinai the centre of the desert, and Mount Zion -the centre of the navel of the earth: these three [20]were created as holy places facing each other. And he blessed the God of gods, who had put the [21]word of the Lord into his mouth, and the Lord for evermore. And he knew that a blessed portion and a blessing had come to Shem and his sons unto the generations for ever -the whole land of Eden and the whole land of the Red Sea, and the whole land of the east and India, and on the Red Sea and the mountains thereof, and all the land of Bashan, and all the land of Lebanon and the islands of Kaftur, and all the mountains of Sanir and 'Amana, and the mountains of Asshur in the north, and all the land of Elam, Asshur, and Babel, and Susan and Ma'edai, and all the mountains of Ararat, and all the region beyond the sea, which is beyond the mountains of Asshur towards the [22]north, a blessed and spacious land, and all that is in it is very good. And for Ham came forth the second portion, beyond the Gihon towards the south to the right of the Garden, and it extends towards the south and it extends to all the mountains of fire, and it extends towards the west to the sea of 'Atel and it extends towards the west till it reaches the sea of Ma'uk -that sea into which [23]everything which is not destroyed descends. And it goes forth towards the north to the limits of Gadir, and it goes forth to the coast of the waters of the sea to the waters of the great sea till it draws near to the river Gihon, and goes along the river Gihon till it reaches the right of the Garden [24]of Eden. And this is the land which came forth for Ham as the portion which he was to occupy [25]for ever for himself and his sons unto their generations for ever. And for Japheth came forth the third portion beyond the river Tina to the north of the outflow of its waters, and it extends north-[26] easterly to the whole region of Gog, and to all the country east thereof. And it extends northerly to the north, and it extends to the mountains of Qelt towards the north, and towards the sea of [27] Ma'uk, and it goes forth to the east of Gadir as far as the region of the waters of the sea. And it extends until it approaches the west of Fara and it returns towards 'Aferag, and it extends easterly [28] to the waters of the sea of Me'at. And it extends to the region of the river Tina in a north-easterly direction until it approaches the boundary of its waters towards the mountain Rafa, and it turns [29] round towards the north. This is the land which came forth for Japheth and his sons as the portion of his inheritance which he should possess for himself and his sons, for their generations for ever; [30] five great islands, and a great land in the north. But it is cold, and the land of Ham is hot, and the land of Shem is neither hot nor cold, but it is of blended cold and heat.

Chapter 9

[1] And Ham divided amongst his sons, and the first portion came forth for Cush towards the east, and to the west of him for Mizraim, and to the west of him for Put, and to the west of him [2] and to the west thereof on the sea for Canaan. And Shem also divided amongst his sons, and the first portion came forth for Ham and his sons, to the east of the river Tigris till it approaches the east, the whole land of India, and on the Red Sea on its coast, and the waters of Dedan, and all the mountains of Mebri and Ela, and all the land of Susan and all that is on the side of Pharnak [3] to the Red Sea and the river Tina. And for Asshur came forth the second Portion, all the land of [4] Asshur and Nineveh and Shinar and to the border of India, and it ascends and skirts the river. And for Arpachshad came forth the third portion, all the land of the region of the Chaldees to the east of the Euphrates, bordering on the Red Sea, and all the waters of the desert close to the tongue of the sea which looks towards Egypt, all the land of Lebanon and Sanir and 'Amana to the border of the [5] Euphrates. And for Aram there came forth the fourth portion, all the land of Mesopotamia between the Tigris and the Euphrates to the north of the Chaldees to the border of the mountains [6] of Asshur and the land of 'Arara. And there came forth for Lud the fifth portion, the mountains of Asshur and all appertaining to them till it reaches the Great Sea, and till it reaches the east of [7], [8] Asshur his brother. And Japheth also divided the land of his inheritance amongst his sons. And the first portion came forth for Gomer to the east from the north side to the river Tina; and in the north there came forth for Magog all the inner portions of the north until it reaches to the sea of [9] Me'at. And for Madai came forth as

his portion that he should posses from the west of his two ¹⁰brothers to the islands, and to the coasts of the islands. And for Javan came forth the fourth ¹¹portion every island and the islands which are towards the border of Lud. And for Tubal there came forth the fifth portion in the midst of the tongue which approaches towards the border of the portion of Lud to the second tongue, to the region beyond the second tongue unto the third tongue. ¹²And for Meshech came forth the sixth portion, all the region beyond the third tongue till it ¹³approaches the east of Gadir. And for Tiras there came forth the seventh portion, four great islands in the midst of the sea, which reach to the portion of Ham and the islands of Kamaturi ¹⁴came out by lot for the sons of Arpachshad as his inheritance. And thus the sons of Noah divided unto their sons in the presence of Noah their father, and he bound them all by an oath, imprecating ¹⁵a curse on every one that sought to seize the portion which had not fallen to him by his lot. And they all said, 'So be it; so be it ' for themselves and their sons for ever throughout their generations till the day of judgment, on which the Lord God shall judge them with a sword and with fire for all the unclean wickedness of their errors, wherewith they have filled the earth with transgression and uncleanness and fornication and sin.

Chapter 10

¹And in the third week of this jubilee the unclean demons began to lead astray the children of ²the sons of Noah, and to make to err and destroy them. And the sons of Noah came to Noah their father, and they told him concerning the demons which were leading astray and blinding and ³slaying his sons' sons. And he prayed before the Lord his God, and said: 'God of the spirits of all flesh, who hast shown mercy unto me And hast saved me and my sons from the waters of the flood, And hast not caused me to perish as Thou didst the sons of perdition; For Thy grace has been great towards me, And great has been Thy mercy to my soul; Let Thy grace be lift up upon my sons, And let not wicked spirits rule over them Lest they should destroy them from the earth. ⁴But do Thou bless me and my sons, that we may increase and Multiply and replenish the earth. ⁵And Thou knowest how Thy Watchers, the fathers of these spirits, acted in my day: and as for these spirits which are living, imprison them and hold them fast in the place of condemnation, and let them not bring destruction on the sons of thy servant, my God; for these are malignant, and ⁶created in order to destroy. And let them not rule over the spirits of the living; for Thou alone canst exercise dominion over them. And let them not have power over the sons of the righteous ⁷,⁸from henceforth and for evermore.' And the

Lord our God bade us to bind all. And the chief of the spirits, Mastema, came and said: 'Lord, Creator, let some of them remain before me, and let them harken to my voice, and do all that I shall say unto them; for if some of them are not left to me, I shall not be able to execute the power of my will on the sons of men; for these are for corruption and leading astray before my judgment, for great is the wickedness of the sons of men.' [9]And He said: Let the tenth part of them remain before him, and let nine parts descend into the [10]place of condemnation.' And one of us He commanded that we should teach Noah all their [11]medicines; for He knew that they would not walk in uprightness, nor strive in righteousness. And we did according to all His words: all the malignant evil ones we bound in the place of condemna-[12]tion and a tenth part of them we left that they might be subject before Satan on the earth. And we explained to Noah all the medicines of their diseases, together with their seductions, how he [13]might heal them with herbs of the earth. And Noah wrote down all things in a book as we instructed him concerning every kind of medicine. Thus the evil spirits were precluded from [14]hurting the sons of Noah. And he gave all that he had written to Shem, his eldest son; for he [15]loved him exceedingly above all his sons. And Noah slept with his fathers, and was buried on [16]Mount Lubar in the land of Ararat. Nine hundred and fifty years he completed in his life, nineteen [17]jubilees and two weeks and five years. And in his life on earth he excelled the children of men save Enoch because of the righteousness, wherein he was perfect. For Enoch's office was ordained for a testimony to the generations of the world, so that he should recount all the deeds of generation [18]unto generation, till the day of judgment. And in the three and thirtieth jubilee, in the first year in the second week, Peleg took to himself a wife, whose name was Lomna the daughter of Sina'ar, and she bare him a son in the fourth year of this week, and he called his name Reu; for he said: 'Behold the children of men have become evil through the wicked purpose of building for themselves [19]a city and a tower in the land of Shinar.' For they departed from the land of Ararat eastward to Shinar; for in his days they built the city and the tower, saying, 'Go to, let us ascend thereby into [20]heaven.' And they began to build, and in the fourth week they made brick with fire, and the bricks served them for stone, and the clay with which they cemented them together was asphalt which [21]comes out of the sea, and out of the fountains of water in the land of Shinar. And they built it: forty and three years were they building it; its breadth was [20]3 bricks, and the height of a brick was the third of one; its height amounted to [54]33 cubits and [2]palms, and the extent of one wall ²²was thirteen stades and of the other thirty stades. And the Lord our God said unto us: Behold, they are one people, and this they begin to do, and now nothing will be withholden from them. Go to, let us go down and confound their language, that they may not understand one another's speech, and they may be dispersed into cities and nations, and one purpose will no longer abide with ²³them till the day of judgment.' And the Lord descended, and we descended with him to see the ²⁴city and the tower which the children of men had built. And he confounded their language, and they no longer understood one another's speech, and they ceased then to build the city and the ²⁵tower. For this reason the whole land of Shinar is called Babel, because the Lord did there confound all the language of the children of men, and from thence they were dispersed into their ²⁶cities, each according to his language and his nation. And the Lord sent a mighty wind against the tower and overthrew it upon the earth, and behold it was between Asshur and Babylon in the ²⁷land of Shinar, and they called its name 'Overthrow'. In the fourth week in the first year in the beginning thereof in the four and thirtieth jubilee, were they dispersed from the land of Shinar. ²⁸And Ham and his sons went into the land which he was to occupy, which he acquired as his portion ²⁹in the land of the south. And Canaan saw the land of Lebanon to the river of Egypt, that it was very good, and he went not into the land of his inheritance to the west that is to the sea, and he dwelt in the land of Lebanon, eastward and westward from the border of Jordan and from the border ³⁰of the sea. And Ham, his father, and Cush and Mizraim his brothers said unto him: 'Thou hast settled in a land which is not thine, and which did not fall to us by lot: do not do so; for if thou dost do so, thou and thy sons will fall in the land and be accursed through sedition; for by sedition ³¹ye have settled, and by sedition will thy children fall, and thou shalt be rooted out for ever. Dwell ³²not in the dwelling of Shem; for to Shem and to his sons did it come by their lot. Cursed art thou, and cursed shalt thou be beyond all the sons of Noah, by the curse by which we bound our- ³³selves by an oath in the presence of the holy judge, and in the presence of Noah our father.' But he did not harken unto them, and dwelt in the land of Lebanon from Hamath to the entering of ³⁴,³⁵Egypt, he and his sons until this day. And for this reason that land is named Canaan. And Japheth and his sons went towards the sea and dwelt in the land of their portion, and Madai saw the land of the sea and it did not please him, and he begged a portion from Ham and Asshur and Arpachshad, his wife's brother, and he dwelt in the land of Media, near to his wife's brother until ³⁶this day. And he called his dwelling-place, and the dwelling-place of his sons, Media, after the name of their father Madai.

Chapter 11

¹And in the thirty-fifth jubilee, in the third week, in the first year thereof, Reu took to himself a wife, and her name was 'Ora, the daughter of 'Ur, the son of Kesed, and she bare him a son, and ²he called his name Seroh, in the seventh year of this week in this jubilee. And the sons of Noah began to war on each other, to take captive and to slay each other, and to shed the blood of men on the earth, and to eat blood, and to build strong cities, and walls, and towers, and individuals began to exalt themselves above the nation, and to found the beginnings of kingdoms, and to go to war people against people, and nation against nation, and city against city, and all began to do evil, and to acquire arms, and to teach their sons war, and they began to capture cities, and to sell ³male and female slaves. And 'Ur, the son of Kesed, built the city of 'Ara of the Chaldees, and called its name after his own name and the name of his father. And they made for themselves molten images, and they worshipped each the idol, the molten image which they had made for themselves, and they began to make graven images and unclean simulacra, and malignant spirits ⁵assisted and seduced them into committing transgression and uncleanness. And the prince Mastema exerted himself to do all this, and he sent forth other spirits, those which were put under his hand, to do all manner of wrong and sin, and all manner of transgression, to corrupt and destroy, ⁶and to shed blood upon the earth. For this reason he called the name of Seroh, Serug, for every one ⁷turned to do all manner of sin and transgression. And he grew up, and dwelt in Ur of the Chaldees, near to the father of his wife's mother, and he worshipped idols, and he took to himself a wife in the thirty-sixth jubilee, in the fifth week, in the first year thereof, and her name was Melka, the daughter ⁸of Kaber, the daughter of his father's brother. And she bare him Nahor, in the first year of this week, and he grew and dwelt in Ur of the Chaldees, and his father taught him the researches of the ⁹Chaldees to divine and augur, according to the signs of heaven. And in the thirty-seventh jubilee in the sixth week, in the first year thereof, he took to himself a wife, and her name was 'Ijaska, the ¹⁰daughter of Nestag of the Chaldees. And she bare him Terah in the seventh year of this week. ¹¹And the prince Mastema sent ravens and birds to devour the seed which was sown in the land, in order to destroy the land, and rob the children of men of their labours. Before they could plough ¹²in the seed, the ravens picked it from the surface of the ground. And for this reason he called his name Terah because the ravens

and the birds reduced them to destitution and devoured their [13] seed. And the years began to be barren, owing to the birds, and they devoured all the fruit of the trees from the trees: it was only with great effort that they could save a little of all the fruit of the [14] earth in their days. And in this thirty-ninth jubilee, in the second week in the first year, Terah took to himself a wife, and her name was 'Edna, the daughter of 'Abram, the daughter of his father's sister. And in the seventh year of this week she bare him a son, and he called his name Abram, [15] by the name of the father of his mother; for he had died before his daughter had conceived a son. [16] And the child began to understand the errors of the earth that all went astray after graven images and after uncleanness, and his father taught him writing, and he was two weeks of years old, and he [17] separated himself from his father, that he might not worship idols with him. And he began to pray to the Creator of all things that He might save him from the errors of the children of men, and that [18] his portion should not fall into error after uncleanness and vileness. And the seed time came for the sowing of seed upon the land, and they all went forth together to protect their seed against the [19] ravens, and Abram went forth with those that went, and the child was a lad of fourteen years. And a cloud of ravens came to devour the seed, and Abram ran to meet them before they settled on the ground, and cried to them before they settled on the ground to devour the seed, and said, ' Descend [20] not: return to the place whence ye came,' and they proceeded to turn back. And he caused the clouds of ravens to turn back that day seventy times, and of all the ravens throughout all the land [21] where Abram was there settled there not so much as one. And all who were with him throughout all the land saw him cry out, and all the ravens turn back, and his name became great in all the [22] land of the Chaldees. And there came to him this year all those that wished to sow, and he went with them until the time of sowing ceased: and they sowed their land, and that year they brought [23] enough grain home and eat and were satisfied. And in the first year of the fifth week Abram taught those who made implements for oxen, the artificers in wood, and they made a vessel above the ground, facing the frame of the plough, in order to put the seed thereon, and the seed fell down therefrom upon the share of the plough, and was hidden in the earth, and they no longer feared the [24] ravens. And after this manner they made vessels above the ground on all the frames of the ploughs, and they sowed and tilled all the land, according as Abram commanded them, and they no longer feared the birds.

Chapter 12

¹And it came to pass in the sixth week, in the seventh year thereof, that Abram said to Terah his ²father, saying, 'Father!' And he said, 'Behold, here am I, my son.' And he said, 'What help and profit have we from those idols which thou dost worship, And before which thou dost bow thyself

³For there is no spirit in them, For they are dumb forms, and a misleading of the heart. Worship them not: ⁴Worship the God of heaven, Who causes the rain and the dew to descend on the earth And does everything upon the earth, and has created everything by His word, And all life is from before His face.⁵Why do ye worship things that have no spirit in them For they are the work of men's hands, and on your shoulders do ye bear them, And ye have no help from them, But they are a great cause of shame to those who make them, And a misleading of the heart to those who worship them: Worship them not.' ⁶ And his father said unto him, I also know it, my son, but what shall I do with a people who have ⁷made me to serve before them And if I tell them the truth, they will slay me; for their soul cleaves to them to worship them and honour them. Keep silent, my son, lest they slay thee.' And ⁹these words he spake to his two brothers, and they were angry with him and he kept silent. And in the fortieth jubilee, in the second week, in the seventh year thereof, Abram took to himself a wife, ¹⁰and her name was Sarai, the daughter of his father, and she became his wife. And Haran, his brother, took to himself a wife in the third year of the third week, and she bare him a son in the ¹¹seventh year of this week, and he called his name Lot. And Nahor, his brother, took to himself ¹²a wife. And in the sixtieth year of the life of Abram, that is, in the fourth week, in the fourth year thereof, Abram arose by night, and burned the house of the idols, and he burned all that was in the ¹³house and no man knew it. And they arose in the night and sought to save their gods from the ¹⁴midst of the fire. And Haran hasted to save them, but the fire flamed over him, and he was burnt in the fire, and he died in Ur of the Chaldees before Terah his father, and they buried him in Ur of ¹⁵the Chaldees. And Terah went forth from Ur of the Chaldees, he and his sons, to go into the land of Lebanon and into the land of Canaan, and he dwelt in the land of Haran, and Abram dwelt with ¹⁶Terah his father in Haran two weeks of years. And in the sixth week, in the fifth year thereof, Abram sat up throughout the night on the new moon of the seventh month to observe the stars from the evening to the morning, in order to see what would be the character of the year with regard ¹⁷to the rains, and he was alone as he sat and observed. And a word came into his heart and he said: All the signs of

the stars, and the signs of the moon and of the sun are all in the hand of the Lord. Why do I search them out [18]if He desires, He causes it to rain, morning and evening; And if He desires, He withholds it, And all things are in his hand.' [19]and he prayed that night and said, 'My God, God Most High, Thou alone art my God, And Thee and Thy dominion have I chosen. And Thou hast created all things, And all things that are the work of thy hands. [20]Deliver me from the hands of evil spirits who have dominion over the thoughts of men's hearts, And let them not lead me astray from Thee, my God. And stablish Thou me and my seed for ever That we go not astray from henceforth and for evermore.' [21]And he said, 'Shall I return unto Ur of the Chaldees who seek my face that I may return to them, am I to remain here in this place The right path before Thee prosper it in the hands of Thy servant that he may fulfil it and that I may not walk in the deceitfulness of my heart, O my God.' [22]And he made an end of speaking and praying, and behold the word of the Lord was sent to him through me, saying: 'Get thee up from thy country, and from thy kindred and from the house of thy father unto a land which I will show thee, and I shall make thee a great and numerous nation. [23]And I will bless thee And I will make thy name great, And thou shalt be blessed in the earth, And in Thee shall all families of the earth be blessed, And I will bless them that bless thee, And curse them that curse thee. [24]And I will be a God to thee and thy son, and to thy son's son, and to all thy seed: fear not, from [25]henceforth and unto all generations of the earth I am thy God.' And the Lord God said: 'Open his mouth and his ears, that he may hear and speak with his mouth, with the language which has been revealed'; for it had ceased from the mouths of all the children of men from the day of the [26]overthrow of Babel. And I opened his mouth, and his ears and his lips, and I began to speak [27]with him in Hebrew in the tongue of the creation. And he took the books of his fathers, and these were written in Hebrew, and he transcribed them, and he began from henceforth to study them, and I made known to him that which he could not understand, and he studied them during the six [28]rainy months. And it came to pass in the seventh year of the sixth week that he spoke to his father and informed him, that he would leave Haran to go into the land of Canaan to see it and [29]return to him. And Terah his father said unto him; Go in peace: may the eternal God make thy path straight. And the Lord be with thee, and protect thee from all evil, And grant unto thee grace, mercy and favour before those who see thee, And may none of the children of men have power over thee to harm thee; Go in peace. [30]And if thou seest a land pleasant to thy eyes to dwell in, then arise and take me to thee and take [31]Lot with thee, the son of Haran thy brother as thine own son: the Lord be with thee. And Nahor thy brother leave with me till thou returnest in peace, and we go with thee all together.'

Chapter 13

[1]And Abram journeyed from Haran, and he took Sarai, his wife, and Lot, his brother Haran's son, to the land of Canaan, and he came into Asshur, and proceeded to Shechem, and dwelt near [2]a lofty oak. And he saw, and, behold, the land was very pleasant from the entering of Hamath to [3]the lofty oak. And the Lord said to him: 'To thee and to thy seed will I give this land.' And [4]he built an altar there, and he offered thereon a burnt sacrifice to the Lord, who had appeared to [5]him. And he removed from thence unto the mountain . . . Bethel on the west and Ai on the [6]east, and pitched his tent there. And he saw and behold, the land was very wide and good, and everything grew thereon -vines and figs and pomegranates, oaks and ilexes, and terebinths and oil trees, and cedars and cypresses and date trees, and all trees of the field, and there was water on the [7]mountains. And he blessed the Lord who had led him out of Ur of the Chaldees, and had brought [8]him to this land. And it came to pass in the first year, in the seventh week, on the new moon of the first month, that he built an altar on this mountain, and called on the name of the Lord: 'Thou, [9]the eternal God, art my God.' And he offered on the altar a burnt sacrifice unto the Lord that He [10]should be with him and not forsake him all the days of his life. And he removed from thence and went towards the south, and he came to Hebron and Hebron was built at that time, and he dwelt there two years, and he went thence into the land of the south, to Bealoth, and there was a famine [11]in the land. And Abram went into Egypt in the third year of the week, and he dwelt in Egypt [12]five years before his wife was torn away from him. Now Tanais in Egypt was at that time built- [13]seven years after Hebron. And it came to pass when Pharaoh seized Sarai, the wife of Abram that the Lord plagued Pharaoh and his house with great plagues because of Sarai, Abram's wife. [14]And Abram was very glorious by reason of possessions in sheep, and cattle, and asses, and horses, and camels, and menservants, and maidservants, and in silver and gold exceedingly. And Lot also [15]his brother's son, was wealthy. And Pharaoh gave back Sarai, the wife of Abram, and he sent him out of the land of Egypt, and he journeyed to the place where he had pitched his tent at the beginning, to the place of the altar, with Ai on the east, and Bethel on the west, and he blessed the [16]Lord his God who had brought him back in peace. And it came to pass in the forty-first jubilee in the third year of

the first week, that he returned to this place and offered thereon a burnt sacrifice, and called on the name of the Lord, and said: 'Thou, the most high God, art my God for ever [17]and ever.' And in the fourth year of this week Lot parted from him, and Lot dwelt in Sodom, and [18]the men of Sodom were sinners exceedingly. And it grieved him in his heart that his brother's [19]son had parted from him; for he had no children. In that year when Lot was taken captive, the Lord said unto Abram, after that Lot had parted from him, in the fourth year of this week: 'Lift up thine eyes from the place where thou art dwelling, northward and southward, and westward and [20]eastward. For all the land which thou seest I will give to thee and to thy seed for ever, and I will make thy seed as the sand of the sea: though a man may number the dust of the earth, yet [21]thy seed shall not be numbered. Arise, walk through the land in the length of it and the breadth of it, and see it all; for to thy seed will I give it.' And Abram went to Hebron, and dwelt there. [22]And in this year came Chedorlaomer, king of Elam, and Amraphel, king of Shinar, and Arioch king of Sellasar, and Tergal, king of nations, and slew the king of Gomorrah, and the king of Sodom [23]fled, and many fell through wounds in the vale of Siddim, by the Salt Sea. And they took captive Sodom and Adam and Zeboim, and they took captive Lot also, the son of Abram's brother, and [24]all his possessions, and they went to Dan. And one who had escaped came and told Abram that [25]his brother's son had been taken captive and Abram armed his household servants . . . . for Abram, and for his seed, a tenth of the first fruits to the Lord, and the Lord ordained it as an ordinance for ever that they should give it to the priests [26]who served before Him, that they should possess it for ever. And to this law there is no limit of days; for He hath ordained it for the generations for ever that they should give to the Lord the tenth of everything, of the seed and of the wine and of the oil and of the cattle and of the sheep. [27],[28]And He gave it unto His priests to eat and to drink with joy before Him. And the king of Sodom came to him and bowed himself before him, and said: 'Our Lord Abram, give unto us the [29]souls which thou hast rescued, but let the booty be thine.' And Abram said unto him: 'I lift up my hands to the Most High God, that from a thread to a shoe-latchet I shall not take aught that is thine lest thou shouldst say, I have made Abram rich; save only what the young men have eaten, and the portion of the men who went with me -Aner, Eschol, and Mamre. These shall take their portion.'

Chapter 14

[1]After these things, in the fourth year of this week, on the new moon of the third month, the word of the Lord

came to Abram in a dream, saying: 'Fear not, Abram; I am thy defender, and ²thy reward will be exceeding great.' And he said: 'Lord, Lord, what wilt thou give me, seeing I go hence childless, and the son of Maseq, the son of my handmaid, is the Dammasek Eliezer: he ³will be my heir, and to me thou hast given no seed.' And he said unto him: 'This man will not ⁴be thy heir, but one that will come out of thine own bowels; he will be thine heir.' And He brought him forth abroad, and said unto him: 'Look toward heaven and number the stars if thou ⁵art able to number them.' And he looked toward heaven, and beheld the stars. And He said ⁶unto him: 'So shall thy seed be.' And he believed in the Lord, and it was counted to him for ⁷righteousness. And He said unto him: 'I am the Lord that brought thee out of Ur of the Chaldees, to give thee the land of the Canaanites to possess it for ever; and I will be God unto thee and to ⁸thy seed after thee.' And he said: 'Lord, Lord, whereby shall I know that I shall inherit it' ⁹And He said unto him: 'Take Me an heifer of three years, and a goat of three years, and a sheep ¹⁰of three years, and a turtle-dove, and a pigeon.' And he took all these in the middle of the month ¹¹and he dwelt at the oak of Mamre, which is near Hebron. And he built there an altar, and sacrificed all these; and he poured their blood upon the altar, and divided them in the midst, and ¹²laid them over against each other; but the birds divided he not. And birds came down upon the ¹³pieces, and Abram drove them away, and did not suffer the birds to touch them. And it came to pass, when the sun had set, that an ecstasy fell upon Abram, and lo ! an horror of great darkness fell upon him, and it was said unto Abram: 'Know of a surety that thy seed shall be a stranger in a land that is not theirs, and they shall bring them into bondage, and afflict them four hundred ¹⁴years. And the nation also to whom they will be in bondage will I judge, and after that they shall ¹⁵come forth thence with much substance. And thou shalt go to thy fathers in peace, and be buried ¹⁶in a good old age. But in the fourth generation they shall return hither; for the iniquity of the ¹⁷Amorites is not yet full.' And he awoke from his sleep, and he arose, and the sun had set; and there was a flame, and behold ! a furnace was smoking, and a flame of fire passed between the ¹⁸pieces. And on that day the Lord made a covenant with Abram, saying: 'To thy seed will I give this land, from the river of Egypt unto the great river, the river Euphrates, the Kenites, the Kenizzites, the Kadmonites, the Perizzites, and the Rephaim, the Phakorites, and the Hivites, and the ¹⁹Amorites, and the Canaanites, and the Girgashites, and the Jebusites. And the day passed, and Abram offered the pieces, and the birds, and their fruit offerings, and their drink offerings, and ²⁰the fire devoured them. And on that day we made a covenant with Abram, according as we had covenanted with Noah in this month; and Abram renewed the festival and ordinance for himself ²¹for ever. And Abram rejoiced, and made all these things known to Sarai his wife; and he believed ²²that he would have seed, but she did not bear. And Sarai advised her husband Abram, and said unto him: 'Go in unto Hagar, my Egyptian maid: it may be that I shall build up seed unto thee ²³by her.' And Abram harkened unto the voice of Sarai his wife, and said unto her, 'Do so.' And Sarai took Hagar, her maid, the Egyptian, and gave her to Abram, her husband, to be his ²⁴wife. And he went in unto her, and she conceived and bare him a son, and he called his name Ishmael, in the fifth year of this week; and this was the eighty-sixth year in the life of Abram.

Chapter 15

¹And in the fifth year of the fourth week of this jubilee, in the third month, in the middle of the ²month, Abram celebrated the feast of the first-fruits of the grain harvest. And he offered new offerings on the altar, the first-fruits of the produce, unto the Lord, an heifer and a goat and a sheep on the altar as a burnt sacrifice unto the Lord; their fruit offerings and their drink offerings he ³offered upon the altar with frankincense. And the Lord appeared to Abram, and said unto him: ⁴'I am God Almighty; approve thyself before me and be thou perfect. And I will make My covenant between Me and thee, and I will multiply thee exceedingly.' And Abram fell on his face, and God talked with him, and said: ⁶'Behold my ordinance is with thee, And thou shalt be the father of many nations. ⁷Neither shall thy name any more be called Abram, But thy name from henceforth, even for ever, shall be Abraham. For the father of many nations have I made thee. And I will make thee very great, And I will make thee into nations, And kings shall come forth from thee. ⁹And I shall establish My covenant between Me and thee, and thy seed after thee, throughout their generations, for an eternal covenant, so that I may be a God unto thee, and to thy seed after thee. ¹⁰the land where thou hast been a sojourner, ¹¹the land of Canaan, that thou mayst possess it for ever, and I will be their God.' And the Lord said unto Abraham: 'And as for thee, do thou keep my covenant, thou and thy seed after thee: and circumcise ye every male among you, and circumcise your foreskins, and it shall be a token of ¹²an eternal covenant between Me and you. And the child on the eighth day ye shall circumcise, every male throughout your generations, him that is born in the house, or whom ye have bought ¹³with money from any stranger, whom ye have acquired who is not of thy seed. He that is born in thy house shall

surely be circumcised, and those whom thou hast bought with money shall be circum- [14]cised, and My covenant shall be in your flesh for an eternal ordinance. And the uncircumcised male who is not circumcised in the flesh of his foreskin on the eighth day, that soul shall be cut off from [15]his people, for he has broken My covenant.' And God said unto Abraham: 'As for Sarai thy wife, [16]her name shall no more be called Sarai, but Sarah shall be her name. And I will bless her, and give thee a son by her, and I will bless him, and he shall become a nation, and kings of nations shall [17]proceed from him.' And Abraham fell on his face, and rejoiced, and said in his heart: 'Shall a son be born to him that is a hundred years old, and shall Sarah, who is ninety years old, bring forth' [18],[19]And Abraham said unto God: 'O that Ishmael might live before thee!' And God said: 'Yea, and Sarah also shall bear thee a son, and thou shalt call his name Isaac, and I will establish My [20]covenant with him, an everlasting covenant, and for his seed after him. And as for Ishmael also have I heard thee, and behold I will bless him, and make him great, and multiply him exceedingly, [21]and he shall beget twelve princes, and I will make him a great nation. But My covenant will [22]I establish with Isaac, whom Sarah shall bear to thee, in these days, in the next year.' And He left [23]off speaking with him, and God went up from Abraham. And Abraham did according as God had said unto him, and he took Ishmael his son, and all that were born in his house, and whom he had [24]bought with his money, every male in his house, and circumcised the flesh of their foreskin. And on the selfsame day was Abraham circumcised, and all the men of his house, , and all those, whom he had bought with money from the children of the stranger, were [25]circumcised with him. This law is for all the generations for ever, and there is no circumcision of the days, and no omission of one day out of the eight days; for it is an eternal ordinance, ordained [26]and written on the heavenly tablets. And every one that is born, the flesh of whose foreskin is not circumcised on the eighth day, belongs not to the children of the covenant which the Lord made with Abraham, but to the children of destruction; nor is there, moreover, any sign on him that he is the Lord's, but he is destined to be destroyed and slain from the earth, and to be rooted out of [27]the earth, for he has broken the covenant of the Lord our God. For all the angels of the presence and all the angels of sanctification have been so created from the day of their creation, and before the angels of the presence and the angels of sanctification He hath sanctified Israel, that they should [28]be with Him and with His holy angels. And do thou command the children of Israel and let them observe the sign of this covenant for their generations as an eternal ordinance, and they will not be ²⁹rooted out of the land. For the command is ordained for a covenant, that they should observe it ³⁰for ever among all the children of Israel. For Ishmael and his sons and his brothers and Esau, the Lord did not cause to approach Him, and he chose them not because they are the children of ³¹Abraham, because He knew them, but He chose Israel to be His people. And He sanctified it, and gathered it from amongst all the children of men; for there are many nations and many peoples, and all are His, and over all hath He placed spirits in authority to lead them astray from Him. ³²But over Israel He did not appoint any angel or spirit, for He alone is their ruler, and He will preserve them and require them at the hand of His angels and His spirits, and at the hand of all His powers in order that He may preserve them and bless them, and that they may be His and He ³³may be theirs from henceforth for ever. And now I announce unto thee that the children of Israel will not keep true to this ordinance, and they will not circumcise their sons according to all this law; for in the flesh of their circumcision they will omit this circumcision of their sons, and all of them, ³⁴sons of Beliar, will leave their sons uncircumcised as they were born. And there will be great wrath from the Lord against the children of Israel, because they have forsaken His covenant and turned aside from His word, and provoked and blasphemed, inasmuch as they do not observe the ordinance of this law; for they have treated their members like the Gentiles, so that they may be removed and rooted out of the land. And there will no more be pardon or forgiveness unto them so that there should be forgiveness and pardon for all the sin of this eternal error.

Chapter 16

¹And on the new moon of the fourth month we appeared unto Abraham, at the oak of Mamre, and we talked with him, and we announced to him that a son would be given to him by Sarah his wife. ²And Sarah laughed, for she heard that we had spoken these words with Abraham, and we admonished ³her, and she became afraid, and denied that she had laughed on account of the words. And we told her the name of her son, as his name is ordained and written in the heavenly tablets i.e. Isaac, ⁴,⁵And that when we returned to her at a set time, she would have conceived a son. And in this month the Lord executed his judgments on Sodom, and Gomorrah, and Zeboim, and all the region of the Jordan, and He burned them with fire and brimstone, and destroyed them until this day, even as I have declared unto thee all their works, that they are wicked and sinners exceedingly, and that they defile themselves and commit

fornication in their flesh, and work uncleanness on the earth. [6] And, in like manner, God will execute judgment on the places where they have done according to [7] the uncleanness of the Sodomites, like unto the judgment of Sodom. But Lot we saved; for God [8] remembered Abraham, and sent him out from the midst of the overthrow. And he and his daughters committed sin upon the earth, such as had not been on the earth since the days of Adam till his [9] time; for the man lay with his daughters. And, behold, it was commanded and engraven concerning all his seed, on the heavenly tablets, to remove them and root them out, and to execute judgment upon them like the judgment of Sodom, and to leave no seed of the man on earth on the day [10] of condemnation. And in this month Abraham moved from Hebron, and departed and dwelt between [11] Kadesh and Shur in the mountains of Gerar. And in the middle of the fifth month he moved from [12] thence, and dwelt at the Well of the Oath. And in the middle of the sixth month the Lord visited [13] Sarah and did unto her as He had spoken and she conceived. And she bare a son in the third month, and in the middle of the month, at the time of which the Lord had spoken to Abraham, on [14] the festival of the first fruits of the harvest, Isaac was born. And Abraham circumcised his son on the eighth day: he was the first that was circumcised according to the covenant which is ordained [15] for ever. And in the sixth year of the fourth week we came to Abraham, to the Well of the Oath, and we appeared unto him as we had told Sarah that we should return to her, and she would have [16] conceived a son. And we returned in the seventh month, and found Sarah with child before us and we blessed him, and we announced to him all the things which had been decreed concerning him, that he should not die till he should beget six sons more, and should see them before he died; but [17] that in Isaac should his name and seed be called: And that all the seed of his sons should be Gentiles, and be reckoned with the Gentiles; but from the sons of Isaac one should become a holy [18] seed, and should not be reckoned among the Gentiles. For he should become the portion of the Most High, and all his seed had fallen into the possession of God, that it should be unto the Lord a people for His possession above all nations and that it should become a kingdom and priests and [19] a holy nation. And we went our way, and we announced to Sarah all that we had told him, and [20] they both rejoiced with exceeding great joy. And he built there an altar to the Lord who had delivered him, and who was making him rejoice in the land of his sojourning, and he celebrated a festival of joy in this month seven days, near the altar which he had built at the Well of the Oath. [21] And he built booths for himself and for his servants on this festival, and he was the first to celebrate ²²the feast of tabernacles on the earth. And during these seven days he brought each day to the altar a burnt offering to the Lord, two oxen, two rams, seven sheep, one he-goat, for a sin offering, ²³that he might atone thereby for himself and for his seed. And, as a thank-offering, seven rams, seven kids, seven sheep, and seven he-goats, and their fruit offerings and their drink offerings; and he burnt all the fat thereof on the altar, a chosen offering unto the Lord for a sweet smelling savour. ²⁴And morning and evening he burnt fragrant substances, frankincense and galbanum, and stackte, and nard, and myrrh, and spice, and costum; all these seven he offered, crushed, mixed together in ²⁵equal parts and pure. And he celebrated this feast during seven days, rejoicing with all his heart and with all his soul, he and all those who were in his house, and there was no stranger with him, ²⁶nor any that was uncircumcised. And he blessed his Creator who had created him in his generation, for He had created him according to His good pleasure; for He knew and perceived that from him would arise the plant of righteousness for the eternal generations, and from him a holy seed, so that it ²⁷should become like Him who had made all things. And he blessed and rejoiced, and he called the ²⁸name of this festival the festival of the Lord, a joy acceptable to the Most High God. And we blessed him for ever, and all his seed after him throughout all the generations of the earth, because ²⁹he celebrated this festival in its season, according to the testimony of the heavenly tablets. For this reason it is ordained on the heavenly tablets concerning Israel, that they shall celebrate the feast of tabernacles seven days with joy, in the seventh month, acceptable before the Lord -a statute for ³⁰ever throughout their generations every year. And to this there is no limit of days; for it is ordained for ever regarding Israel that they should celebrate it and dwell in booths, and set wreaths upon ³¹their heads, and take leafy boughs, and willows from the brook. And Abraham took branches of palm trees, and the fruit of goodly trees, and every day going round the altar with the branches seven times a day in the morning, he praised and gave thanks to his God for all things in joy.

Chapter 17

¹And in the first year of the fifth week Isaac was weaned in this jubilee, and Abraham made ²a great banquet in the third month, on the day his son Isaac was weaned. And Ishmael, the son of Hagar, the Egyptian, was before the face of Abraham, his father, in his place, and Abraham rejoiced ³and blessed God because he had seen his sons and had not died childless. And he remembered the

words which He had spoken to him on the day on which Lot had parted from him, and he rejoiced because the Lord had given him seed upon the earth to inherit the earth, and he blessed with all his [4]mouth the Creator of all things. And Sarah saw Ishmael playing and dancing, and Abraham rejoicing with great joy, and she became jealous of Ishmael and said to Abraham, 'Cast out this [5]bondwoman and her son; for the son of this bondwoman will not be heir with my son, Isaac.' And the thing was grievous in Abraham's sight, because of his maidservant and because of his son, [6]that he should drive them from him. And God said to Abraham 'Let it not be grievous in thy sight, because of the child and because of the bondwoman; in all that Sarah hath said unto thee, [7]harken to her words and do them; for in Isaac shall thy name and seed be called. But as for [8]the son of this bondwoman I will make him a great nation, because he is of thy seed.' And Abraham rose up early in the morning, and took bread and a bottle of water, and placed them on the shoulders [9]of Hagar and the child, and sent her away. And she departed and wandered in the wilderness of Beersheba, and the water in the bottle was spent, and the child thirsted, and was not able to go on, [10]and fell down. And his mother took him and cast him under an olive tree, and went and sat her down over against him, at the distance of a bow-shot; for she said, 'Let me not see the death of my [11]child,' and as she sat she wept. And an angel of God, one of the holy ones, said unto her, 'Why weepest thou, Hagar Arise take the child, and hold him in thine hand; for God hath heard thy [12]voice, and hath seen the child.' And she opened her eyes, and she saw a well of water, and she went and filled her bottle with water, and she gave her child to drink, and she arose and went towards [13]the wilderness of Paran. And the child grew and became an archer, and God was with him, and his [14]mother took him a wife from among the daughters of Egypt. And she bare him a son, and he called [15]his name Nebaioth; for she said, 'The Lord was nigh to me when I called upon him.' And it came to pass in the seventh week, in the first year thereof, in the first month in this jubilee, on the twelfth of this month, there were voices in heaven regarding Abraham, that he was faithful in all that He [16]told him, and that he loved the Lord, and that in every affliction he was faithful. And the prince Mastema came and said before God, 'Behold, Abraham loves Isaac his son, and he delights in him above all things else; bid him offer him as a burnt-offering on the altar, and Thou wilt see if he will do this command, and Thou wilt know if he is faithful in everything wherein Thou dost try him. [17]And the Lord knew that Abraham was faithful in all his afflictions; for He had tried him through his country and with famine, and had tried him with the wealth of kings, and had tried him again through his wife, when she was torn from him, and with circumcision; and had tried him through [18]Ishmael and Hagar, his maid-servant, when he sent them away. And in everything wherein He had tried him, he was found faithful, and his soul was not impatient, and he was not slow to act; for he was faithful and a lover of the Lord.

Chapter 18

[1],[2]And God said to him, 'Abraham, Abraham'; and he said, Behold, here am I.' And he said, Take thy beloved son whom thou lovest, even Isaac, and go unto the high country, and offer him [3]on one of the mountains which I will point out unto thee.' And he rose early in the morning and saddled his ass, and took his two young men with him, and Isaac his son, and clave the wood of the [4]burnt offering, and he went to the place on the third day, and he saw the place afar off. And he came to a well of water, and he said to his young men, 'Abide ye here with the ass, and I and the [5]lad shall go yonder, and when we have worshipped we shall come again to you.' And he took the wood of the burnt-offering and laid it on Isaac his son, and he took in his hand the fire and the [6]knife, and they went both of them together to that place. And Isaac said to his father, 'Father;' and he said, 'Here am I, my son.' And he said unto him, 'Behold the fire, and the knife, and the [7]wood; but where is the sheep for the burnt-offering, father' And he said, 'God will provide for himself a sheep for a burnt-offering, my son.' And he drew near to the place of the mount of [8]God. And he built an altar, and he placed the wood on the altar, and bound Isaac his son, and placed him on the wood which was upon the altar, and stretched forth his hand to take the knife [9]to slay Isaac his son. And I stood before him, and before the prince Mastema, and the Lord said, 'Bid him not to lay his hand on the lad, nor to do anything to him, for I have shown that he fears [10]the Lord.' And I called to him from heaven, and said unto him: 'Abraham, Abraham;' and he [11]was terrified and said: 'Behold, here am I.' And I said unto him: 'Lay not thy hand upon the lad, neither do thou anything to him; for now I have shown that thou fearest the Lord, and hast [12]not withheld thy son, thy first-born son, from me.' And the prince Mastema was put to shame; and Abraham lifted up his eyes and looked, and, behold a ram caught . . . by his horns, and Abraham [13]went and took the ram and offered it for a burnt-offering in the stead of his son. And Abraham called that place 'The Lord hath seen', so that it is said the Lord hath seen: that is [14]Mount Sion. And the Lord called Abraham by his name a second time from heaven, as he caused [15]us to appear to speak to

him in the name of the Lord. And he said: 'By Myself have I sworn, saith the Lord, because thou hast done this thing, And hast not withheld thy son, thy beloved son, from Me, That in blessing I will bless thee, and in multiplying I will multiply thy seed As the stars of heaven, And as the sand which is on the seashore. And thy seed shall inherit the cities of its enemies, [16] And in thy seed shall all nations of the earth be blessed; because thou hast obeyed My voice, And I have shown to all that thou art faithful unto Me in all that I have said unto thee: Go in peace.' [17] And Abraham went to his young men, and they arose and went together to Beersheba, and Abraham [18] dwelt by the Well of the Oath. And he celebrated this festival every year, seven days with joy, and he called it the festival of the Lord according to the seven days during which he went and [19] returned in peace. And accordingly has it been ordained and written on the heavenly tablets regarding Israel and its seed that they should observe this festival seven days with the joy of festival.

Chapter 19

[1] And in the first year of the first week in the forty-second jubilee, Abraham returned and dwelt [2] opposite Hebron, that is Kirjath Arba, two weeks of years. And in the first year of the third week [3] of this jubilee the days of the life of Sarah were accomplished, and she died in Hebron. And Abraham went to mourn over her and bury her, and we tried him to see if his spirit were patient and he were not indignant in the words of his mouth; and he was found patient in this, and was not [4] disturbed. For in patience of spirit he conversed with the children of Heth, to the intent that they [5] should give him a place in which to bury his dead. And the Lord gave him grace before all who saw him, and he besought in gentleness the sons of Heth, and they gave him the land of the double [6] cave over against Mamre, that is Hebron, for four hundred pieces of silver. And they besought him saying, We shall give it to thee for nothing; but he would not take it from their hands for nothing, for he gave the price of the place, the money in full, and he bowed down before them twice, and after [7] this he buried his dead in the double cave. And all the days of the life of Sarah were one hundred and twenty-seven years, that is, two jubilees and four weeks and one year: these are the days of the [8] years of the life of Sarah. This is the tenth trial wherewith Abraham was tried, and he was found [9] faithful, patient in spirit. And he said not a single word regarding the rumour in the land how that God had said that He would give it to him and to his seed after him, and he begged a place there to bury his dead; for he was found faithful, and was recorded on the heavenly tablets as the friend of [10] God. And in the fourth year thereof

he took a wife for his son Isaac and her name was Rebecca the sister of Laban and daughter of Bethuel; and Bethuel was the son of Melca, who was the wife of Nahor, the brother of Abraham. [11]And Abraham took to himself a third wife, and her name was Keturah, from among the daughters of his household servants, for Hagar had died before Sarah. And she bare him six sons, Zimram, [12]and Jokshan, and Medan, and Midian, and Ishbak, and Shuah, in the two weeks of years. And in [13]the sixth week, in the second year thereof, Rebecca bare to Isaac two sons, Jacob and Esau, and Jacob was a smooth and upright man, and Esau was fierce, a man of the field, and hairy, and Jacob [14]dwelt in tents. And the youths grew, and Jacob learned to write; but Esau did not learn, for he [15]was a man of the field and a hunter, and he learnt war, and all his deeds were fierce. And Abraham [16]loved Jacob, but Isaac loved Esau. And Abraham saw the deeds of Esau, and he knew that in Jacob should his name and seed be called; and he called Rebecca and gave commandment regarding [17]Jacob, for he knew that she too loved Jacob much more than Esau. And he said unto her: my daughter, watch over my son Jacob, For he shall be in my stead on the earth, And for a blessing in the midst of the children of men, And for the glory of the whole seed of Shem. [18]For I know that the Lord will choose him to be a people for possession unto Himself, above all [19]peoples that are upon the face of the earth. And behold, Isaac my son loves Esau more than Jacob, but I see that thou truly lovest Jacob.[20]Add still further to thy kindness to him, And let thine eyes be upon him in love; For he shall be a blessing unto us on the earth from henceforth unto all generations of the earth. [21]Let thy hands be strong And let thy heart rejoice in thy son Jacob; For I have loved him far beyond all my sons. He shall be blessed for ever, And his seed shall fill the whole earth. [22]If a man can number the sand of the earth, His seed also shall be numbered. [23]And all the blessings wherewith the Lord hath blessed me and my seed shall belong to Jacob and [24]his seed alway. And in his seed shall my name be blessed, and the name of my fathers, Shem, and [25]Noab, and Enoch, and Mahalalel, and Enos, and Seth, and Adam. And these shall serve to lay the foundations of the heaven, And to strengthen the earth, And to renew all the luminaries which are in the firmament. [26]And he called Jacob before the eyes of Rebecca his mother, and kissed him, and blessed him, and [27]said: 'Jacob, my beloved son, whom my soul loveth, may God bless thee from above the firmament, and may He give thee all the blessings wherewith He blessed Adam, and Enoch, and Noah, and Shem; and all the things of which He told me, and all the things which He promised to give me, may he cause to cleave to thee and to thy seed for ever, according to the days of heaven above the [28]earth. And the Spirits of Mastema shall not rule over thee or over thy seed to turn thee from the [29]Lord, who is thy God from henceforth for ever. And may the Lord God be a father to thee and [30]thou the first-born son, and to the people alway. Go in peace, my son.' And they both went forth [31]together from Abraham. And Rebecca loved Jacob, with all her heart and with all her soul, very much more than Esau; but Isaac loved Esau much more than Jacob.

Chapter 20

[1]And in the forty-second jubilee, in the first year of the seventh week, Abraham called Ishmael, [2]and his twelve sons, and Isaac and his two sons, and the six sons of Keturah, and their sons. And he commanded them that they should observe the way of the Lord; that they should work righteousness, and love each his neighbour, and act on this manner amongst all men; that they should each [3]so walk with regard to them as to do judgment and righteousness on the earth. That they should circumcise their sons, according to the covenant which He had made with them, and not deviate to the right hand or the left of all the paths which the Lord had commanded us; and that we should keep ourselves from all fornication and uncleanness, and renounce from amongst us all fornication and [4]uncleanness. And if any woman or maid commit fornication amongst you, burn her with fire and let them not commit fornication with her after their eyes and their heart; and let them not take to themselves wives from the daughters of Canaan; for the seed of Canaan will be rooted out of [5]the land. And he told them of the judgment of the giants, and the judgment of the Sodomites, how they had been judged on account of their wickedness, and had died on account of their fornication, and uncleanness, and mutual corruption through fornication. [6]'And guard yourselves from all fornication and uncleanness, And from all pollution of sin, lest ye make our name a curse, And your whole life a hissing, and all your sons to be destroyed by the sword, And ye become accursed like Sodom, And all your remnant as the sons of Gomorrah. [7]I implore you, my sons, love the God of heaven And cleave ye to all His commandments. And walk not after their idols, and after their uncleannesses, [8]And make not for yourselves molten or graven gods; for they are vanity, And there is no spirit in them; for they are work of men's hands, And all who trust in them, trust in nothing. [9]Serve them not, nor worship them, But serve ye the most high God, and worship Him continually: And hope for His countenance always, And work uprightness and righteousness before Him, that He may have pleasure in you and grant you His mercy, And

send rain upon you morning and evening, and bless all your works which ye have wrought upon the earth, And bless thy bread and thy water, and bless the fruit of thy womb and the fruit of thy land, And the herds of thy cattle, and the flocks of thy sheep. [10]And ye will be for a blessing on the earth, And all nations of the earth will desire you, and bless your sons in my name, That they may be blessed as I am. [11]And he gave to Ishmael and to his sons, and to the sons of Keturah, gifts, and sent them away [12]from Isaac his son, and he gave everything to Isaac his son. And Ishmael and his sons, and the sons of Keturah and their sons, went together and dwelt from Paran to the entering in of Babylon in [13]all the land which is towards the East facing the desert. And these mingled with each other, and their name was called Arabs, and Ishmaelites.

Chapter 21

[1]And in the sixth year of the seventh week of this jubilee Abraham called Isaac his son, and commanded him: saying, 'I am become old, and know not the day of my death, and am full of my [2]days. And behold, I am one hundred and seventy-five years old, and throughout all the days of my life I have remembered the Lord, and sought with all my heart to do His will, and to walk uprightly [3]in all His ways. My soul has hated idols, [4]given my heart and spirit that I might observe to do the will of Him who created me. For He is the living God, and He is holy and faithful, and He is righteous beyond all, and there is with Him no accepting of men's persons and no accepting of gifts; for God is righteous, and executeth judg- [5]ment on all those who transgress His commandments and despise His covenant. And do thou, my son, observe His commandments and His ordinances and His judgments, and walk not after the [6]abominations and after the graven images and after the molten images. And eat no blood at all of [7]animals or cattle, or of any bird which flies in the heaven. And if thou dost slay a victim as an acceptable peace offering, slay ye it, and pour out its blood upon the altar, and all the fat of the offering offer on the altar with fine flour and the meat offering mingled with oil, with its drink offering -offer them all together on the altar of burnt offering; it is a sweet savour before the Lord. [8]And thou wilt offer the fat of the sacrifice of thank offerings on the fire which is upon the altar, and the fat which is on the belly, and all the fat on the inwards and the two kidneys, and all the fat that [9]is upon them, and upon the loins and liver thou shalt remove, together with the kidneys. And offer all these for a sweet savour acceptable before the Lord, with its meat-offering and with its drink- [10]offering, for a sweet savour, the bread of the offering unto the Lord. And eat its meat on that day

and on the second day, and let not the sun on the second day go down upon it till it is eaten, and let nothing be left over for the third day; for it is not acceptable for it is not approved and let it no longer be eaten, and all who eat thereof will bring sin upon themselves; for thus I have found it written in the books of my forefathers, and in the words of Enoch, and in the words of Noah. [11]And on all thy oblations thou shalt strew salt, and let not the salt of the covenant be lacking in all [12]thy oblations before the Lord. And as regards the wood of the sacrifices, beware lest thou bring other wood for the altar in addition to these: cypress, bay, almond, fir, pine, cedar, savin, fig, olive, [13]myrrh, laurel, aspalathus. And of these kinds of wood lay upon the altar under the sacrifice, such as have been tested as to their appearance, and do not lay thereon any split or dark wood, but hard and clean, without fault, a sound and new growth; and do not lay thereon old wood, for its [14]fragrance is gone for there is no longer fragrance in it as before. Besides these kinds of wood there is none other that thou shalt place on the altar, for the fragrance is dispersed, and the smell of its [15]fragrance goes not up to heaven. Observe this commandment and do it, my son, that thou mayst [16]be upright in all thy deeds. And at all times be clean in thy body, and wash thyself with water before thou approachest to offer on the altar, and wash thy hands and thy feet before thou drawest [17]near to the altar; and when thou art done sacrificing, wash again thy hands and thy feet. And let no blood appear upon you nor upon your clothes; be on thy guard, my son, against blood, be on thy [18]guard exceedingly; cover it with dust. And do not eat any blood for it is the soul; eat no blood whatever. And take no gifts for the blood of man, lest it be shed with impunity, without judgment; for it is the blood that is shed that causes the earth to sin, and the earth cannot be cleansed from the [20]blood of man save by the blood of him who shed it. And take no present or gift for the blood of man: blood for blood, that thou mayest be accepted before the Lord, the Most High God; for He is the defence of the good: and that thou mayest be preserved from all evil, and that He may save thee from every kind of death. [21]I see, my son, That all the works of the children of men are sin and wickedness, And all their deeds are uncleanness and an abomination and a pollution, And there is no righteousness with them. [22]Beware, lest thou shouldest walk in their ways And tread in their paths, And sin a sin unto death before the Most High God. Else He will hide His face from thee And give thee back into the hands of thy transgression, And root thee out of the land, and thy seed likewise from under heaven, And thy name and thy seed shall perish from the whole earth. [23]Turn away from all their deeds and all their uncleanness, And observe the ordinance of the Most High God, And do His will and be upright in all things. ²⁴And He will bless thee in all thy deeds, And will raise up from thee a plant of righteousness through all the earth, throughout all generations of the earth, And my name and thy name shall not be forgotten under heaven for ever. ²⁵Go, my son in peace. May the Most High God, my God and thy God, strengthen thee to do His will, And may He bless all thy seed and the residue of thy seed for the generations for ever, with all righteous blessings, That thou mayest be a blessing on all the earth.' ²⁶And he went out from him rejoicing.

Chapter 22

¹And it came to pass in the first week in the forty-fourth jubilee, in the second year, that is, the year in which Abraham died, that Isaac and Ishmael came from the Well of the Oath to celebrate the feast of weeks -that is, the feast of the first fruits of the harvest-to Abraham, their ²father, and Abraham rejoiced because his two sons had come. For Isaac had many possessions in ³Beersheba, and Isaac was wont to go and see his possessions and to return to his father. And in those days Ishmael came to see his father, and they both came together, and Isaac offered a sacrifice ⁴for a burnt offering, and presented it on the altar of his father which he had made in Hebron. And he offered a thank offering and made a feast of joy before Ishmael, his brother: and Rebecca made new cakes from the new grain, and gave them to Jacob, her son, to take them to Abraham, his father, from the first fruits of the land, that he might eat and bless the Creator of all things before he died. ⁵And Isaac, too, sent by the hand of Jacob to Abraham a best thank offering, that he might eat and ⁶drink. And he eat and drank, and blessed the Most High God, Who hath created heaven and earth, Who hath made all the fat things of the earth, And given them to the children of men That they might eat and drink and bless their Creator. ⁷'And now I give thanks unto Thee, my God, because thou hast caused me to see this day: behold, I am one hundred three score and fifteen years, an old man and full of days, and all my days have ⁸been unto me peace. The sword of the adversary has not overcome me in all that Thou hast given ⁹me and my children all the days of my life until this day. My God, may Thy mercy and Thy peace be upon Thy servant, and upon the seed of his sons, that they may be to Thee a chosen nation and an inheritance from amongst all the nations of the earth from henceforth unto all the days of the ¹⁰generations of the earth, unto all the ages.' And he called Jacob and said: 'My son Jacob, may the God of all bless thee and strengthen thee to do righteousness, and His will before Him, and may He choose thee and thy

seed that ye may become a people for His inheritance according to His will ¹¹alway. And do thou, my son, Jacob, draw near and kiss me.' And he drew near and kissed him, and he said: 'Blessed be my son Jacob And all the sons of God Most High, unto all the ages: may God give unto thee a seed of righteousness; And some of thy sons may He sanctify in the midst of the whole earth; may nations serve thee, And all the nations bow themselves before thy seed. ¹²Be strong in the presence of men, And exercise authority over all the seed of Seth. Then thy ways and the ways of thy sons will be justified, So that they shall become a holy nation. ¹³May the Most High God give thee all the blessings Wherewith He has blessed me And wherewith He blessed Noah and Adam; May they rest on the sacred head of thy seed from generation to generation for ever. ¹⁴And may He cleanse thee from all unrighteousness and impurity, That thou mayest be forgiven all the transgressions; which thou hast committed ignorantly. And may He strengthen thee, And bless thee. And mayest thou inherit the whole earth, ¹⁵And may He renew His covenant with thee. That thou mayest be to Him a nation for His inheritance for all the ages, And that He may be to thee and to thy seed a God in truth and righteousness throughout all the days of the earth. ¹⁶And do thou, my son Jacob, remember my words, And observe the commandments of Abraham, thy father: separate thyself from the nations, And eat not with them: And do not according to their works, And become not their associate; for their works are unclean, And all their ways are a Pollution and an abomination and uncleanness. ¹⁷They offer their sacrifices to the dead And they worship evil spirits, and they eat over the graves, And all their works are vanity and nothingness. ¹⁸They have no heart to understand And their eyes do not see what their works are, and how they err in saying to a piece of wood: 'Thou art my God,' And to a stone: 'Thou art my Lord and thou art my deliverer.' And they have no heart. ¹⁹And as for thee, my son Jacob, May the Most High God help thee And the God of heaven bless thee And remove thee from their uncleanness and from all their error. ²⁰Be thou ware, my son Jacob, of taking a wife from any seed of the daughters of Canaan; For all his seed is to be rooted out of the earth. ²¹For, owing to the transgression of Ham, Canaan erred, And all his seed shall be destroyed from off the earth and all the residue thereof, And none springing from him shall be saved on the day of judgment. ²²And as for all the worshippers of idols and the profane b There shall be no hope for them in the land of the living; c And there shall be no remembrance of them on the earth; c For they shall descend into Sheol, d And into the place of condemnation shall they go, as the children of Sodom were taken away from the earth So will all those who worship idols be taken away. ²³Fear not, my son Jacob, And be not dismayed, O son of Abraham: may the Most High God preserve thee from destruction, And from all the paths of error may he deliver thee. ²⁴This house have I built for myself that I might put my name upon it in the earth: it is given to thee and to thy seed for ever, and it will be named the house of Abraham; it is given to thee and to thy seed for ever; for thou wilt build my house and establish my name before God for ever: thy seed and thy name will stand throughout all generations of the earth.' ²⁵,²⁶And he ceased commanding him and blessing him. And the two lay together on one bed, and Jacob slept in the bosom of Abraham, his father's father and he kissed him seven times, and his ²⁷affection and his heart rejoiced over him. And he blessed him with all his heart and said: 'The Most High God, the God of all, and Creator of all, who brought me forth from Ur of the Chaldees that he might give me this land to inherit it for ever, and that I might establish a holy seed-blessed ²⁸be the Most High for ever.' And he blessed Jacob and said: 'My son, over whom with all my heart and my affection I rejoice, may Thy grace and Thy mercy be lift up upon him and upon his seed ²⁹alway. And do not forsake him, nor set him at nought from henceforth unto the days of eternity, and may Thine eyes be opened upon him and upon his seed, that Thou mayst preserve him, and ³⁰bless him, and mayest sanctify him as a nation for Thine inheritance; And bless him with all Thy blessings from henceforth unto all the days of eternity, and renew Thy covenant and Thy grace with him and with his seed according to all Thy good pleasure unto all the generations of the earth.'

Chapter 23

¹And he placed two fingers of Jacob on his eyes, and he blessed the God of gods, and he covered his face and stretched out his feet and slept the sleep of eternity, and was gathered to his fathers. ²And notwithstanding all this Jacob was lying in his bosom, and knew not that Abraham, his father's ³father, was dead. And Jacob awoke from his sleep, and behold Abraham was cold as ice, and he ⁴said 'Father, father'; but there was none that spake, and he knew that he was dead. And he arose from his bosom and ran and told Rebecca, his mother; and Rebecca went to Isaac in the night, and told him; and they went together, and Jacob with them, and a lamp was in his hand, and ⁵when they had gone in they found Abraham lying dead. And Isaac fell on the face of his father ⁶and wept and kissed him. And the voices were heard in the house of Abraham, and Ishmael his son arose, and went to Abraham his father, and wept over

Abraham his father, he and all the house [7]of Abraham, and they wept with a great weeping. And his sons Isaac and Ishmael buried him in the double cave, near Sarah his wife, and they wept for him forty days, all the men of his house, and Isaac and Ishmael, and all their sons, and all the sons of Keturah in their places; and the days of [8]weeping for Abraham were ended. And he lived three jubilees and four weeks of years, one hundred [9]and seventy-five years, and completed the days of his life, being old and full of days. For the days of the forefathers, of their life, were nineteen jubilees; and after the Flood they began to grow less than nineteen jubilees, and to decrease in jubilees, and to grow old quickly, and to be full of their days by reason of manifold tribulation and the wickedness of their ways, with the exception of [10]Abraham. For Abraham was perfect in all his deeds with the Lord, and well-pleasing in righteousness all the days of his life; and behold, he did not complete four jubilees in his life, when he had [11]grown old by reason of the wickedness, and was full of his days. And all the generations which shall arise from this time until the day of the great judgment shall grow old quickly, before they complete two jubilees, and their knowledge shall forsake them by reason of their old age Land all their know- [12]ledge shall vanish away. And in those days, if a man live a jubilee and a-half of years, they shall say regarding him: 'He has lived long, and the greater part of his days are pain and sorrow and [13]tribulation, and there is no peace: For calamity follows on calamity, and wound on wound, and tribulation on tribulation, and evil tidings on evil tidings, and illness on illness, and all evil judgments such as these, one with another, illness and overthrow, and snow and frost and ice, and fever, and chills, and torpor, and famine, and death, and sword, and captivity, and all kinds of calamities and [14]pains.' And all these shall come on an evil generation, which transgresses on the earth: their works [15]are uncleanness and fornication, and pollution and abominations. Then they shall say: 'The days of the forefathers were many even, unto a thousand years, and were good; but behold, the days of our life, if a man has lived many, are three score years and ten, and, if he is strong, four score years, [16]and those evil, and there is no peace in the days of this evil generation.' And in that generation the sons shall convict their fathers and their elders of sin and unrighteousness, and of the words of their mouth and the great wickednesses which they perpetrate, and concerning their forsaking the covenant which the Lord made between them and Him, that they should observe and do all His commandments and His ordinances and all His laws, without departing either to the right hand or the left.

[17] For all have done evil, and every mouth speaks iniquity and all their works are an uncleanness and [18] an abomination, and all their ways are pollution, uncleanness and destruction. Behold the earth shall be destroyed on account of all their works, and there shall be no seed of the vine, and no oil; for their works are altogether faithless, and they shall all perish together, beasts and cattle and birds, and [19] all the fish of the sea, on account of the children of men. And they shall strive one with another, the young with the old, and the old with the young, the poor with the rich, the lowly with the great, and the beggar with the prince, on account of the law and the covenant; for they have forgotten commandment, and covenant, and feasts, and months, and Sabbaths, and jubilees, and all judgments. [20] And they shall stand swords and war to turn them back into the way; but they shall [21] not return until much blood has been shed on the earth, one by another. And those who have escaped shall not return from their wickedness to the way of righteousness, but they shall all exalt themselves to deceit and wealth, that they may each take all that is his neighbour's, and they shall name the great name, but not in truth and not in righteousness, and they shall defile the holy of [22] holies with their uncleanness and the corruption of their pollution. And a great punishment shall befall the deeds of this generation from the Lord, and He will give them over to the sword and to [23] judgment and to captivity, and to be plundered and devoured. And He will wake up against them the sinners of the Gentiles, who have neither mercy nor compassion, and who shall respect the person of none, neither old nor young, nor any one, for they are more wicked and strong to do evil than all the children of men. And they shall use violence against Israel and transgression against Jacob, And much blood shall be shed upon the earth, And there shall be none to gather and none to bury. [24] In those days they shall cry aloud, And call and pray that they may be saved from the hand of the sinners, the Gentiles; But none shall be saved. [25] And the heads of the children shall be white with grey hair, And a child of three weeks shall appear old like a man of one hundred years, And their stature shall be destroyed by tribulation and oppression. [26] And in those days the children shall begin to study the laws, And to seek the commandments, And to return to the path of righteousness. [27] And the days shall begin to grow many and increase amongst those children of men Till their days draw nigh to one thousand years. And to a greater number of years than before was the number of the days. [28] And there shall be no old man Nor one who is satisfied with his days, For all shall be as children and youths. [29] And all their days they shall complete and live

in peace and in joy, And there shall be no Satan nor any evil destroyer; For all their days shall be days of blessing and healing. [30] And at that time the Lord will heal His servants, And they shall rise up and see great peace, And drive out their adversaries. And the righteous shall see and be thankful, And rejoice with joy for ever and ever, And shall see all their judgments and all their curses on their enemies. [31] And their bones shall rest in the earth, And their spirits shall have much joy, And they shall know that it is the Lord who executes judgment, And shows mercy to hundreds and thousands and to all that love Him [32] and do thou, Moses, write down these words; for thus are they written, and they record them on the heavenly tablets for a testimony for the generations for ever.

Chapter 24

[1] And it came to pass after the death of Abraham, that the Lord blessed Isaac his son, and he arose from Hebron and went and dwelt at the Well of the Vision in the first year of the third week [2] of this jubilee, seven years. And in the first year of the fourth week a famine began in the land, [3] besides the first famine, which had been in the days of Abraham. And Jacob sod lentil pottage, and Esau came from the field hungry. And he said to Jacob his brother: 'Give me of this red pottage.' And Jacob said to him: 'Sell to me thy primogeniture, this birthright and I will give [4] thee bread, and also some of this lentil pottage.' And Esau said in his heart: 'I shall die; of [5] what profit to me is this birthright 'And he said to Jacob: 'I give it to thee.' And Jacob said: [6] 'Swear to me, this day,' and he sware unto him. And Jacob gave his brother Esau bread and pottage, and he eat till he was satisfied, and Esau despised his birthright; for this reason was Esau's name [7] called Edom, on account of the red pottage which Jacob gave him for his birthright. And Jacob became [8] the elder, and Esau was brought down from his dignity. And the famine was over the land, and Isaac departed to go down into Egypt in the second year of this week, and went to the king of the Philis- [9] tines to Gerar, unto Abimelech. And the Lord appeared unto him and said unto him: 'Go not down into Egypt; dwell in the land that I shall tell thee of, and sojourn in this land, and I will [10] be with thee and bless thee. For to thee and to thy seed will I give all this land, and I will establish My oath which I sware unto Abraham thy father, and I will multiply thy seed as the [11] stars of heaven, and will give unto thy seed all this land. And in thy seed shall all the nations of the earth be blessed, because thy father obeyed My voice, and kept My charge and My commandments, and My laws, and My ordinances, and My covenant; and now obey My voice and dwell in [12],[13] this land.' And he dwelt in Gelar three weeks of years. And Abimelech

charged concerning him, and concerning all that was his, saying: 'Any man that shall touch him or aught that is his shall ¹⁴surely die.' And Isaac waxed strong among the Philistines, and he got many possessions, oxen ¹⁵and sheep and camels and asses and a great household. And he sowed in the land of the Philistines and brought in a hundred-fold, and Isaac became exceedingly great, and the Philistines envied him. ¹⁶Now all the wells which the servants of Abraham had dug during the life of Abraham, the Philistines ¹⁷had stopped them after the death of Abraham, and filled them with earth. And Abimelech said unto Isaac: 'Go from us, for thou art much mightier than we', and Isaac departed thence in ¹⁸the first year of the seventh week, and sojourned in the valleys of Gerar. And they digged again the wells of water which the servants of Abraham, his father, had digged, and which the Philistines had closed after the death of Abraham his father, and he called their names as Abraham his father ¹⁹had named them. And the servants of Isaac dug a well in the valley, and found living water, and the shepherds of Gerar strove with the shepherds of Isaac, saying: 'The water is ours'; and Isaac ²⁰called the name of the well 'Perversity', because they had been perverse with us. And they dug a second well, and they strove for that also, and he called its name 'Enmity'. And he arose from thence and they digged another well, and for that they strove not, and he called the name of it 'Room', and Isaac said: 'Now the Lord hath made room for us, and we have increased in the ²¹land.' And he went up from thence to the Well of the Oath in the first year of the first week in the ²²forty-fourth jubilee. And the Lord appeared to him that night, on the new moon of the first month, and said unto him: 'I am the God of Abraham thy father; fear not, for I am with thee, and shall bless thee and shall surely multiply thy seed as the sand of the earth, for the sake of Abraham my ²³servant.' And he built an altar there, which Abraham his father had first built, and he called upon ²⁴the name of the Lord, and he offered sacrifice to the God of Abraham his father. And they digged ²⁵a well and they found living water. And the servants of Isaac digged another well and did not find water, and they went and told Isaac that they had not found water, and Isaac said: 'I have sworn ²⁶this day to the Philistines and this thing has been announced to us.' And he called the name of that place the Well of the Oath; for there he had sworn to Abimelech and Ahuzzath his friend and ²⁷Phicol the prefect Or his host. And Isaac knew that day that under constraint he had sworn to them ²⁸to make peace with them. And Isaac on that day cursed the Philistines and said: 'Cursed be the Philistines unto the day of wrath and indignation from the midst of all nations; may God make them a derision and a curse and an object of wrath and indignation in the hands of the sinners the [29]Gentiles and in the hands of the Kittim. And whoever escapes the sword of the enemy and the Kittim, may the righteous nation root out in judgment from under heaven; for they shall be the enemies and foes of my children throughout their generations upon the earth. [30]And no remnant shall be left to them, Nor one that shall be saved on the day of the wrath of judgment; For destruction and rooting out and expulsion from the earth is the whole seed of the Philistines reserved, And there shall no longer be left for these Caphtorim a name or a seed on the earth. [31]For though he ascend unto heaven, Thence shall he be brought down, and though he make himself strong on earth, Thence shall he be dragged forth, and though he hide himself amongst the nations, Even from thence shall he be rooted out; and though he descend into Sheol, There also shall his condemnation be great, And there also he shall have no peace. [32]And if he go into captivity, By the hands of those that seek his life shall they slay him on the way, And neither name nor seed shall be left to him on all the earth; For into eternal malediction shall he depart.' [33]And thus is it written and engraved concerning him on the heavenly tablets, to do unto him on the day of judgment, so that he may be rooted out of the earth.

Chapter 25

[1]And in the second year of this week in this jubilee, Rebecca called Jacob her son, and spake unto him, saying: 'My son, do not take thee a wife of the daughters of Canaan, as Esau, thy brother, who took him two wives of the daughters of Canaan, and they have embittered my soul with all their unclean deeds: for all their deeds are fornication and lust, and there is no righteousness with them, [2]for their deeds are evil. And I, my son, love thee exceedingly, and my heart and my affection [3]bless thee every hour of the day and watch of the night. And now, my son, hearken to my voice, and do the will of thy mother, and do not take thee a wife of the daughters of this land, but only of the house of my father, and of my father's kindred. Thou shalt take thee a wife of the house of my father, and the Most High God will bless thee, and thy children shall be a righteous generation and [4]a holy seed.' And then spake Jacob to Rebecca, his mother, and said unto her: 'Behold, mother, I am nine weeks of years old, and I neither know nor have I touched any woman, nor have I betrothed [5]myself to any, nor even think of taking me a wife of the daughters of Canaan. For I remember, mother, the words of Abraham, our father, for he commanded me not to take a wife of the daughters [6]of Canaan, but to take me a wife from

the seed of my father's house and from my kindred. I have heard before that daughters have been born to Laban, thy brother, and I have set my heart on them [7]to take a wife from amongst them. And for this reason I have guarded myself in my spirit against sinning or being corrupted in all my ways throughout all the days of my life; for with regard to lust [8]and fornication, Abraham, my father, gave me many commands. And, despite all that he has commanded me, these two and twenty years my brother has striven with me, and spoken frequently to me and said: 'My brother, take to wife a sister of my two wives'; but I refuse to do as he has done. [9]I swear before thee, mother, that all the days of my life I will not take me a wife from the daughters [10]of the seed of Canaan, and I will not act wickedly as my brother has done. Fear not, mother; be [11]assured that I shall do thy will and walk in uprightness, and not corrupt my ways for ever.' And thereupon she lifted up her face to heaven and extended the fingers of her hands, and opened her mouth and blessed the Most High God, who had created the heaven and the earth, and she gave Him [12]thanks and praise. And she said: 'Blessed be the Lord God, and may His holy name be blessed for ever and ever, who has given me Jacob as a pure son and a holy seed; for he is Thine, and Thine [13]shall his seed be continually and throughout all the generations for evermore. Bless him, O Lord, [14]and place in my mouth the blessing of righteousness, that I may bless him.' And at that hour, when the spirit of righteousness descended into her mouth, she placed both her hands on the head of Jacob, and said: [15]Blessed art thou, Lord of righteousness and God of the ages And may He bless thee beyond all the generations of men. May He give thee, my Son, the path of righteousness, And reveal righteousness to thy seed. [16]And may He make thy sons many during thy life, And may they arise according to the number of the months of the year. And may their sons become many and great beyond the stars of heaven, And their numbers be more than the sand of the sea. [17]And may He give them this goodly land -as He said He would give it to Abraham and to his seed after him alway- And may they hold it as a possession for ever. [18]And may I see born unto thee, my son, blessed children during my life, And a blessed and holy seed may all thy seed be. [19]And as thou hast refreshed thy mother's spirit during her life, The womb of her that bare thee blesses thee thus, my affection and my breasts bless thee And my mouth and my tongue praise thee greatly. [20]Increase and spread over the earth, And may thy seed be perfect in the joy of heaven and earth for ever; and may thy seed rejoice, And on the great day of peace may it have peace. [21]And may thy name and thy seed endure to all the ages, And may the Most High God be their God, And may the God of righteousness dwell with them, And by them may His sanctuary be built unto all the ages. [22] Blessed be he that blesseth thee, And all flesh that curseth thee falsely, may it be cursed.' [23] And she kissed him, and said to him; 'May the Lord of the world love thee As the heart of thy mother and her affection rejoice in thee and bless thee.' And she ceased from blessing.

Chapter 26

[1] And in the seventh year of this week Isaac called Esau, his elder Son, and said unto him: ' I am [2] old, my son, and behold my eyes are dim in seeing, and I know not the day of my death. And now take thy hunting weapons thy quiver and thy bow, and go out to the field, and hunt and catch me venison, my son, and make me savoury meat, such as my soul loveth, and bring it to me that I may [3] eat, and that my soul may bless thee before I die.' But Rebecca heard Isaac speaking to Esau. [4,5] And Esau went forth early to the field to hunt and catch and bring home to his father. And Rebecca called Jacob, her son, and said unto him: 'Behold, I heard Isaac, thy father, speak unto Esau, thy brother, saying: "Hunt for me, and make me savoury meat, and bring it to me that [6] I may eat and bless thee before the Lord before I die." And now, my son, obey my voice in that which I command thee: Go to thy flock and fetch me two good kids of the goats, and I will make them savoury meat for thy father, such as he loves, and thou shalt bring it to thy father that he [7] may eat and bless thee before the Lord before he die, and that thou mayst be blessed.' And Jacob said to Rebecca his mother: 'Mother, I shall not withhold anything which my father would eat, and which would please him: only I fear, my mother, that he will recognise my voice and wish to touch [8] me. And thou knowest that I am smooth, and Esau, my brother, is hairy, and I shall appear before his eyes as an evildoer, and shall do a deed which he had not commanded me, and he will be [9] wroth with me, and I shall bring upon myself a curse, and not a blessing.' And Rebecca, his [10] mother, said unto him: 'Upon me be thy curse, my son, only obey my voice.' And Jacob obeyed the voice of Rebecca, his mother, and went and fetched two good and fat kids of the goats, and [11] brought them to his mother, and his mother made them ~savoury meat~ such as he loved. And Rebecca took the goodly rainment of Esau, her elder son, which was with her in the house, and she clothed Jacob, her younger son, with them, and she put the skins of the kids upon his hands and on [12] the exposed parts of his neck. And she gave the meat and the bread which she had prepared into [13] the hand of her son Jacob. And Jacob went in to his father and said: 'I am thy son: I have done

according as thou badest me: arise and sit and eat of that which I have caught, father, that thy soul ¹⁴,¹⁵may bless me.' And Isaac said to his son: 'How hast thou found so quickly, my son 'And Jacob ¹⁶said: 'Because the Lord thy God caused me to find.' And Isaac said unto him: Come near, that ¹⁷I may feel thee, my son, if thou art my son Esau or not.' And Jacob went near to Isaac, his father, ¹⁸and he felt him and said: 'The voice is Jacob's voice, but the hands are the hands of Esau,' and he discerned him not, because it was a dispensation from heaven to remove his power of perception and ¹⁹Isaac discerned not, for his hands were hairy as his brother Esau's, so that he blessed him. And he said: 'Art thou my son Esau ' and he said: 'I am thy son': and he said, 'Bring near to me that ²⁰I may eat of that which thou hast caught, my son, that my soul may bless thee.' And he brought ²¹near to him, and he did eat, and he brought him wine and he drank. And Isaac, his father, said unto ²²him: 'Come near and kiss me, my son. And he came near and kissed him. And he smelled the smell of his raiment, and he blessed him and said: 'Behold, the smell of my son is as the smell of a full field which the Lord hath blessed. ²³And may the Lord give thee of the dew of heaven And of the dew of the earth, and plenty of corn and oil: let nations serve thee, And peoples bow down to thee. ²⁴Be lord over thy brethren, And let thy mother's sons bow down to thee; and may all the blessings wherewith the Lord hath blessed me and blessed Abraham, my father; Be imparted to thee and to thy seed for ever: cursed be he that curseth thee, And blessed be he that blesseth thee.' ²⁵And it came to pass as soon as Isaac had made an end of blessing his son Jacob, and Jacob had gone ²⁶forth from Isaac his father he hid himself and Esau, his brother, came in from his hunting. And he also made savoury meat, and brought it to his father, and said unto his father: 'Let my father ²⁷arise, and eat of my venison that thy soul may bless me.' And Isaac, his father, said unto him: 'Who art thou 'And he said unto him: 'I am thy first born, thy son Esau: I have done as thou hast ²⁸commanded me.' And Isaac was very greatly astonished, and said: 'Who is he that hath hunted and caught and brought it to me, and I have eaten of all before thou camest, and have blessed him: ²⁹and he shall be blessed, and all his seed for ever.' And it came to pass when Esau heard the words of his father Isaac that he cried with an exceeding great and bitter cry, and said unto his father: ³⁰'Bless me, even me also, father.' And he said unto him: 'Thy brother came with guile, and hath taken away thy blessing.' And he said: 'Now I know why his name is named Jacob: behold, he hath supplanted me these two times: he took away my birth-right, and now he hath taken away ³¹my blessing.' And he said: 'Hast thou not reserved a blessing for me, father' and Isaac answered and said unto Esau: ³¹'Behold, I have made him thy lord, And all his brethren have I given to him for servants, And with plenty of corn and wine and oil have I strengthened him: And what now shall I do for thee, my son' ³²And Esau said to Isaac, his father: 'Hast thou but one blessing, O father Bless me, even me also, father: ' ³³And Esau lifted up his voice and wept. And Isaac answered and said unto him: 'Behold, far from the dew of the earth shall be thy dwelling, And far from the dew of heaven from above. ³⁴And by thy sword wilt thou live, And thou wilt serve thy brother. And it shall come to pass when thou becomest great, And dost shake his yoke from off thy neck, Thou shalt sin a complete sin unto death, And thy seed shall be rooted out from under heaven.' ³⁵And Esau kept threatening Jacob because of the blessing wherewith his father blessed him, and he: said in his heart: 'May the days of mourning for my father now come, so that I may slay my brother Jacob.'

Chapter 27

¹And the words of Esau, her elder son, were told to Rebecca in a dream, and Rebecca sent and ²called Jacob her younger son, and said unto him: 'Behold Esau thy brother will take vengeance on ³thee so as to kill thee. Now, therefore, my son, obey my voice, and arise and flee thou to Laban, my brother, to Haran, and tarry with him a few days until thy brother's anger turns away, and he remove his anger from thee, and forget all that thou hast done; then I will send and fetch thee from ⁴,⁵thence.' And Jacob said: 'I am not afraid; if he wishes to kill me, I will kill him.' But she said ⁶unto him: 'Let me not be bereft of both my sons on one day.' And Jacob said to Rebecca his mother: 'Behold, thou knowest that my father has become old, and does not see because his eyes are dull, and if I leave him it will be evil in his eyes, because I leave him and go away from you, and my father will be angry, and will curse me. I will not go; when he sends me, then only will I go.' ⁷,⁸And Rebecca said to Jacob: 'I will go in and speak to him, and he will send thee away.' And Rebecca went in and said to Isaac: 'I loathe my life because of the two daughters of Heth, whom Esau has taken him as wives; and if Jacob take a wife from among the daughters of the land such ⁹as these, for what purpose do I further live, for the daughters of Canaan are evil.' And Isaac called ¹⁰Jacob and blessed him, and admonished him and said unto him: 'Do not take thee a wife of any of the daughters of Canaan; arise and go to Mesopotamia, to the house of Bethuel, thy mother's father, ¹¹and take thee a wife from thence of the daughters of Laban, thy mother's brother. And God Almighty bless thee

and increase and multiply thee that thou mayest become a company of nations, and give thee the blessings of my father Abraham, to thee and to thy seed after thee, that thou mayest inherit the land of thy sojournings and all the land which God gave to Abraham: go, my [12]son, in peace.' And Isaac sent Jacob away, and he went to Mesopotamia, to Laban the son of [13]Bethuel the Syrian, the brother of Rebecca, Jacob's mother. And it came to pass after Jacob had [14]arisen to go to Mesopotamia that the spirit of Rebecca was grieved after her son, and she wept. And Isaac said to Rebecca: 'My sister, weep not on account of Jacob, my son; for he goeth in peace, and [15]in peace will he return. The Most High God will preserve him from all evil, and will be with him; [16]for He will not forsake him all his days; For I know that his ways will be prospered in all things [17]wherever he goes, until he return in peace to us, and we see him in peace. Fear not on his account, my sister, for he is on the upright path and he is a perfect man: and he is faithful and will not perish. [18],[19]Weep not.' And Isaac comforted Rebecca on account of her son Jacob, and blessed him. And Jacob went from the Well of the Oath to go to Haran on the first year of the second week in the forty-fourth jubilee, and he came to Luz on the mountains, that is, Bethel, on the new moon of the first month of this week, and he came to the place at even and turned from the way to the west of the [20]road that night: and he slept there; for the sun had set. And he took one of the stones of that [21]place and laid under the tree, and he was journeying alone, and he slept. And he dreamt that night, and behold a ladder set up on the earth, and the top of it reached to heaven, and behold, the angels of the Lord ascended and descended on it: and behold, the Lord stood upon it. [22]And he spake to Jacob and said: 'I am the Lord God of Abraham, thy father, and the God of [23]Isaac; the land whereon thou art sleeping, to thee will I give it, and to thy seed after thee. And thy seed shall be as the dust of the earth, and thou shalt increase to the west and to the east, to the [24]north and the south, and in thee and in thy seed shall all the families of the nations be blessed. And behold, I will be with thee, and will keep thee whithersoever thou goest, and I will bring thee again into this land in peace; for I will not leave thee until I do everything that I told thee of.' [25]And Jacob awoke from his sleep, and said, 'Truly this place is the house of the Lord, and I knew it not.' And he was afraid and said: 'Dreadful is this place which is none other than the house of [26]God, and this is the gate of heaven.' And Jacob arose early in the morning, and took the stone which he had put under his head and set it up as a pillar for a sign, and he poured oil upon the top of it. And he called the name of that place Bethel; but the name of the place was Luz at the first.

²⁷And Jacob vowed a vow unto the Lord, saying: 'If the Lord will be with me, and will keep me in this way that I go, and give me bread to eat and raiment to put on, so that I come again to my father's house in peace, then shall the Lord be my God, and this stone which I have set up as a pillar for a sign in this place, shall be the Lord's house, and of all that thou givest me, I shall give the tenth to thee, my God.'

Chapter 28

¹And he went on his journey, and came to the land of the east, to Laban, the brother of Rebecca, ²and he was with him, and served him for Rachel his daughter one week. And in the first year of the third week he said unto him: 'Give me my wife, for whom I have served thee seven years '; and ³Laban said unto Jacob: 'I will give thee thy wife.' And Laban made a feast, and took Leah his elder daughter, and gave her to Jacob as a wife, and gave her Zilpah his handmaid for an hand- ⁴maid; and Jacob did not know, for he thought that she was Rachel. And he went in unto her, and behold, she was Leah; and Jacob was angry with Laban, and said unto him: 'Why hast thou dealt thus with me Did not I serve thee for Rachel and not for Leah Why hast thou wronged me ⁵Take thy daughter, and I will go; for thou hast done evil to me.' For Jacob loved Rachel more than Leah; for Leah's eyes were weak, but her form was very handsome; but Rachel had beautiful ⁶eyes and a beautiful and very handsome form. And Laban said to Jacob: 'It is not so done in our country, to give the younger before the elder.' And it is not right to do this; for thus it is ordained and written in the heavenly tablets, that no one should give his younger daughter before the elder; but the elder, one gives first and after her the younger -and the man who does so, they set down guilt against him in heaven, and none is righteous that does this thing, for this deed is evil before the ⁷Lord. And command thou the children of Israel that they do not this thing; let them neither take ⁸nor give the younger before they have given the elder, for it is very wicked. And Laban said to Jacob: 'Let the seven days of the feast of this one pass by, and I shall give thee Rachel, that thou mayst serve me another seven years, that thou mayst pasture my sheep as thou didst in the former week.' And on the day when the seven days of the feast of Leah had passed, Laban gave Rachel to Jacob, that he might serve him another seven years, and he gave to Rachel Bilhah, the sister of ¹⁰Zilpah, as a handmaid. And he served yet other seven years for Rachel, for Leah had been given ¹¹to him for nothing. And the Lord opened the womb of Leah, and she conceived and bare Jacob a son, and he called his name Reuben, on the fourteenth day of the ninth month, in the first

year of [12]the third week. But the womb of Rachel was closed, for the Lord saw that Leah was hated and [13]Rachel loved. And again Jacob went in unto Leah, and she conceived, and bare Jacob a second son, and he called his name Simeon, on the twenty-first of the tenth month, and in the third year of this [14]week. And again Jacob went in unto Leah, and she conceived, and bare him a third son, and he [15]called his name Levi, in the new moon of the first month in the sixth year of this week. And again Jacob went in unto her, and she conceived, and bare him a fourth son, and he called his name Judah, [16]on the fifteenth of the third month, in the first year of the fourth week. And on account of all this Rachel envied Leah, for she did not bear, and she said to Jacob: 'Give me children'; and Jacob [17]said: 'Have I withheld from thee the fruits of thy womb Have I forsaken thee' And when Rachel saw that Leah had borne four sons to Jacob, Reuben and Simeon and Levi and Judah, she said unto [18]him: 'Go in unto Bilhah my handmaid, and she will conceive, and bear a son unto me.' And she gave him Bilhah her handmaid to wife. And he went in unto her, and she conceived, and bare him a son, and he called his name Dan, on the ninth of the sixth month, in the sixth year of the [19]third week. And Jacob went in again unto Bilhah a second time, and she conceived, and bare Jacob another son, and Rachel called his name Napthali, on the fifth of the seventh month, in the [20]second year of the fourth week. And when Leah saw that she had become sterile and did not bear, she envied Rachel, and she also gave her handmaid Zilpah to Jacob to wife, and she conceived, and bare a son, and Leah called his name Gad, on the twelfth of the eighth month, in the third year of [21]the fourth week. And he went in again unto her, and she conceived, and bare him a second son, and Leah called his name Asher, on the second of the eleventh month, in the fifth year of the fourth [22]week. And Jacob went in unto Leah, and she conceived, and bare a son, and she called his name Issachar, on the fourth of the fifth month, in the fourth year of the fourth week, and she gave him [23]to a nurse. And Jacob went in again unto her, and she conceived, and bare two children, a son and a daughter, and she called the name of the son Zabulon, and the name of the daughter Dinah, [24]in the seventh of the seventh month, in the sixth year of the fourth week. And the Lord was gracious to Rachel, and opened her womb, and she conceived, and bare a son, and she called his [25]name Joseph, on the new moon of the fourth month, in the sixth year in this fourth week. And in the days when Joseph was born, Jacob said to Laban: 'Give me my wives and sons, and let me go to my father Isaac, and let me make me an house; for I have completed the years in which I [26]have served thee for thy two daughters, and I will go to the house of my father.' And Laban said to Jacob: 'Tarry with me for thy wages, and pasture my flock for me again, and take thy wages.' ^{27}And they agreed with one another that he should give him as his wages those of the lambs and kids ^{28}which were born black and spotted and white, these were to be his wages. And all the sheep brought forth spotted and speckled and black, variously marked, and they brought forth again lambs like themselves, and all that were spotted were Jacob's and those which were not were ^{29}Laban's. And Jacob's possessions multiplied exceedingly, and he possessed oxen and sheep and ^{30}asses and camels, and menservants and maid-servants. And Laban and his sons envied Jacob, and Laban took back his sheep from him, and he observed him with evil intent.

Chapter 29

^{1}And it came to pass when Rachel had borne Joseph, that Laban went to shear his sheep; for they ^{2}were distant from him a three days' journey. And Jacob saw that Laban was going to shear his sheep, and Jacob called Leah and Rachel, and spake kindly unto them that they should come with ^{3}him to the land of Canaan. For he told them how he had seen everything in a dream, even all that He had spoken unto him that he should return to his father's house, and they said: 'To every place ^{4}whither thou goest we will go with thee.' And Jacob blessed the God of Isaac his father, and the God of Abraham his father's father, and he arose and mounted his wives and his children, and took all his possessions and crossed the river, and came to the land of Gilead, and Jacob hid his intention ^{5}from Laban and told him not. And in the seventh year of the fourth week Jacob turned his face toward Gilead in the first month, on the twenty-first thereof. And Laban pursued after him and ^{6}overtook Jacob in the mountain of Gilead in the third month, on the thirteenth thereof. And the Lord did not suffer him to injure Jacob; for he appeared to him in a dream by night. And Laban ^{7}spake to Jacob. And on the fifteenth of those days Jacob made a feast for Laban, and for all who came with him, and Jacob sware to Laban that day, and Laban also to Jacob, that neither should ^{8}cross the mountain of Gilead to the other with evil purpose. And he made there a heap for ^{9}a witness; wherefore the name of that place is called: 'The Heap of Witness,' after this heap. But before they used to call the land of Gilead the land of the Rephaim; for it was the land of the Rephaim, and the Rephaim were born there, giants whose height was ten, nine, eight down to ^{10}seven cubits. And their habitation was from the land of the children of Ammon to Mount Hermon, ^{11}and the seats of their kingdom were Karnaim and Ashtaroth, and Edrei, and Misur, and

Beon. And the Lord destroyed them because of the evil of their deeds; for they were very malignant, and the Amorites dwelt in their stead, wicked and sinful, and there is no people to-day which has wrought [12]to the full all their sins, and they have no longer length of life on the earth. And Jacob sent away Laban, and he departed into Mesopotamia, the land of the East, and Jacob returned to the land of [13]Gilead. And he passed over the Jabbok in the ninth month, on the eleventh thereof. And on that day Esau, his brother, came to him, and he was reconciled to him, and departed from him unto [14]the land of Seir, but Jacob dwelt in tents. And in the first year of the fifth week in this jubilee he crossed the Jordan, and dwelt beyond the Jordan, and he pastured his sheep from the sea of the [15]heap unto Bethshan, and unto Dothan and unto the forest of Akrabbim. And he sent to his father Isaac of all his substance, clothing, and food, and meat, and drink, and milk, and butter, and [16]cheese, and some dates of the valley. And to his mother Rebecca also four times a year, between the times of the months, between ploughing and reaping, and between autumn and the rain season [17]and between winter and spring, to the tower of Abraham. For Isaac had returned from the Well of the Oath and gone up to the tower of his father Abraham, and he dwelt there apart from his son [18]Esau. For in the days when Jacob went to Mesopotamia, Esau took to himself a wife Mahalath, the daughter of Ishmael, and he gathered together all the flocks of his father and his wives, and went [19]Up and dwelt on Mount Seir, and left Isaac his father at the Well of the Oath alone. And Isaac went up from the Well of the Oath and dwelt in the tower of Abraham his father on the mountains [20]of Hebron, And thither Jacob sent all that he did send to his father and his mother from time to time, all they needed, and they blessed Jacob with all their heart and with all their soul.

Chapter 30

[1]And in the first year of the sixth week he went up to Salem, to the east of Shechem, in peace, in [2]the fourth month. And there they carried off Dinah, the daughter of Jacob, into the house of Shechem, the son of Hamor, the Hivite, the prince of the land, and he lay with her and defiled her, [3]and she was a little girl, a child of twelve years. And he besought his father and her brothers that she might be given to him to wife. And Jacob and his sons were wroth because of the men of Shechem; for they had defiled Dinah, their sister, and they spake to them with evil intent and dealt [4]deceitfully with them and beguiled them. And Simeon and Levi came unexpectedly to Shechem and executed judgment on all the men of Shechem, and slew all the men whom they found in it, and left not a single one remaining in it:

The Book of Jubilees 75

they slew all in torments because they had dishonoured ⁵their sister Dinah. And thus let it not again be done from henceforth that a daughter of Israel be defiled; for judgment is ordained in heaven against them that they should destroy with the sword ⁶all the men of the Shechemites because they had wrought shame in Israel. And the Lord delivered them into the hands of the sons of Jacob that they might exterminate them with the sword and execute judgment upon them, and that it might not thus again be done in Israel that a virgin of ⁷Israel should be defiled. And if there is any man who wishes in Israel to give his daughter or his sister to any man who is of the seed of the Gentiles he shall surely die, and they shall stone him with stones; for he hath wrought shame in Israel; and they shall burn the woman with fire, because ⁸she has dishonoured the name of the house of her father, and she shall be rooted out of Israel. And let not an adulteress and no uncleanness be found in Israel throughout all the days of the generations of the earth; for Israel is holy unto the Lord, and every man who has defiled it shall surely die: ⁹they shall stone him with stones. For thus has it been ordained and written in the heavenly tablets regarding all the seed of Israel: he who defileth it shall surely die, and he shall be stoned with ¹⁰stones. And to this law there is no limit of days, and no remission, nor any atonement: but the man who has defiled his daughter shall be rooted out in the midst of all Israel, because he has given ¹¹of his seed to Moloch, and wrought impiously so as to defile it. And do thou, Moses, command the children of Israel and exhort them not to give their daughters to the Gentiles, and not to take for ¹²their sons any of the daughters of the Gentiles, for this is abominable before the Lord. For this reason I have written for thee in the words of the Law all the deeds of the Shechemites, which they wrought against Dinah, and how the sons of Jacob spake, saying: 'We will not give our daughter ¹³to a man who is uncircumcised; for that were a reproach unto us.' And it is a reproach to Israel, to those who live, and to those that take the daughters of the Gentiles; for this is unclean and ¹⁴abominable to Israel. And Israel will not be free from this uncleanness if it has a wife of the daughters of the Gentiles, or has given any of its daughters to a man who is of any of the Gentiles. ¹⁵For there will be plague upon plague, and curse upon curse, and every judgment and plague and curse will come : if he do this thing, or hide his eyes from those who commit uncleanness, or those who defile the sanctuary of the Lord, or those who profane His holy name, then will the ¹⁶whole nation together be judged for all the uncleanness and profanation of this man. And there will be no respect of persons and no consideration of persons and no receiving at his hands of fruits and offerings and burnt-offerings and fat, nor the fragrance of sweet savour, so as to accept it: and [17]so fare every man or woman in Israel who defiles the sanctuary. For this reason I have commanded thee, saying: 'Testify this testimony to Israel: see how the Shechemites fared and their sons: how they were delivered into the hands of two sons of Jacob, and they slew them under tortures, and it [18]was reckoned unto them for righteousness, and it is written down to them for righteousness. And the seed of Levi was chosen for the priesthood, and to be Levites, that they might minister before the Lord, as we, continually, and that Levi and his sons may be blessed for ever; for he was zealous [19]to execute righteousness and judgment and vengeance on all those who arose against Israel. And so they inscribe as a testimony in his favour on the heavenly tablets blessing and righteousness before [20]the God of all: And we remember the righteousness which the man fulfilled during his life, at all periods of the year; until a thousand generations they will record it, and it will come to him and to his descendants after him, and he has been recorded on the heavenly tablets as a friend and a righteous [21]man. All this account I have written for thee, and have commanded thee to say to the children of Israel, that they should not commit sin nor transgress the ordinances nor break the covenant which [22]has been ordained for them, but that they should fulfil it and be recorded as friends. But if they transgress and work uncleanness in every way, they will be recorded on the heavenly tablets as adversaries, and they will be destroyed out of the book of life, and they will be recorded in the book of [23]those who will be destroyed and with those who will be rooted out of the earth. And on the day when the sons of Jacob slew Shechem a writing was recorded in their favour in heaven that they had executed righteousness and uprightness and vengeance on the sinners, and it was written for a blessing. [24]And they brought Dinah, their sister, out of the house of Shechem, and they took captive everything that was in Shechem, their sheep and their oxen and their asses, and all their wealth, and all their [25]flocks, and brought them all to Jacob their father. And he reproached them because they had put the city to the sword for he feared those who dwelt in the land, the Canaanites and the Perizzites. [26]And the dread of the Lord was upon all the cities which are around about Shechem, and they did not rise to pursue after the sons of Jacob; for terror had fallen upon them.

Chapter 31

[1]And on the new moon of the month Jacob spake to all the people of his house. saying: 'Purify yourselves and change your garments, and let us arise

and go up to Bethel, where I vowed a vow to Him on the day when I fled from the face of Esau my brother, because he has been with me and ²brought me into this land in peace, and put ye away the strange gods that are among you.' And they gave up the strange gods and that which was in their ears and which was on their necks and the idols which Rachel stole from Laban her father she gave wholly to Jacob. And he burnt and brake them to pieces and destroyed them, and hid them under an oak which is in the land of ³Shechem. And he went up on the new moon of the seventh month to Bethel. And he built an altar at the place where he had slept, and he set up a pillar there, and he sent word to his father ⁴Isaac to come to him to his sacrifice, and to his mother Rebecca. And Isaac said: 'Let my son ⁵Jacob come, and let me see him before I die.' And Jacob went to his father Isaac and to his mother Rebecca, to the house of his father Abraham, and he took two of his sons with him, Levi and Judah, and he came to his father Isaac and to his mother Rebecca. ⁶And Rebecca came forth from the tower to the front of it to kiss Jacob and embrace him; for her spirit had revived when she heard: 'Behold Jacob thy son has come'; and she kissed ⁷him. And she saw his two sons, and she recognised them, and said unto him: 'Are these thy sons, my son' and she embraced them and kissed them, and blessed them, saying: 'In you shall the ⁸seed of Abraham become illustrious, and ye shall prove a blessing on the earth.' And Jacob went in to Isaac his father, to the chamber where he lay, and his two sons were with him, and he took the hand of his father, and stooping down he kissed him, and Isaac clung to the neck of Jacob his son, ⁹and wept upon his neck. And the darkness left the eyes of Isaac, and he saw the two sons of Jacob, ¹⁰Levi, and Judah, and he said: 'Are these thy sons, my son for they are like thee.' And he said unto him that they were truly his sons: 'And thou hast truly seen that they are truly my sons'. ¹¹And they came near to him, and he turned and kissed them and embraced them both together. ¹²And the spirit of prophecy came down into his mouth, and he took Levi by his right hand and ¹³Judah by his left. And he turned to Levi first, and began to bless him first, and said unto him: May the God of all, the very Lord of all the ages, bless thee and thy children throughout all the ¹⁴ages. And may the Lord give to thee and to thy seed greatness and great glory, and cause thee and thy seed, from among all flesh, to approach Him to serve in His sanctuary as the angels of the presence and as the holy ones. Even as they, shall the seed of thy sons be for glory and greatness ¹⁵and holiness, and may He make them great unto all the ages. And they shall be judges and princes, and chiefs of all the seed of the sons of Jacob; they shall speak the word of the Lord in righteousness, And they shall judge all His judgments in righteousness. And they shall declare My ways to Jacob And My paths to Israel. The blessing of the Lord shall be given in their mouths To bless all the seed of the beloved. [16]Thy mother has called thy name Levi, And justly has she called thy name; thou shalt be joined to the Lord And be the companion of all the sons of Jacob; let His table be thine, And do thou and thy sons eat thereof; and may thy table be full unto all generations, And thy food fail not unto all the ages. [17]And let all who hate thee fall down before thee, And let all thy adversaries be rooted out and perish; and blessed be he that blesses thee, And cursed be every nation that curses thee.' [18]And to Judah he said: 'May the Lord give thee strength and power To tread down all that hate thee; A prince shalt thou be, thou and one of thy sons, over the sons of Jacob; may thy name and the name of thy sons go forth and traverse every land and region. Then shall the Gentiles fear before thy face, and all the nations shall quake And all the peoples shall quake. In thee shall be the help of Jacob, And in thee be found the salvation of Israel. [20]And when thou sittest on the throne of honour of thy righteousness There shall be great peace for all the seed of the sons of the beloved; blessed be he that blesseth thee, And all that hate thee and afflict thee and curse thee Shall be rooted out and destroyed from the earth and be accursed.' [21]And turning he kissed him again and embraced him, and rejoiced greatly; for he had seen the [22]sons of Jacob his son in very truth. And he went forth from between his feet and fell down and bowed down to him, and he blessed them and rested there with Isaac his father that night, and they [23]eat and drank with joy. And he made the two sons of Jacob sleep, the one on his right hand and the [24]other on his left, and it was counted to him for righteousness. And Jacob told his father everything during the night, how the Lord had shown him great mercy, and how he had prospered him in all [25]his ways, and protected him from all evil. And Isaac blessed the God of his father Abraham, who [26]had not withdrawn his mercy and his righteousness from the sons of his servant Isaac. And in the morning Jacob told his father Isaac the vow which he had vowed to the Lord, and the vision which he had seen, and that he had built an altar, and that everything was ready for the sacrifice to be [27]made before the Lord as he had vowed, and that he had come to set him on an ass. And Isaac said unto Jacob his son: 'I am not able to go with thee; for I am old and not able to bear the way: go, my son, in peace; for I am one hundred and sixty-five years this day; I am no longer able to [28]journey; set thy mother on an ass and let her go with thee. And I know, my son, that thou hast come on my account, and may this day be blessed on which thou hast seen me alive, and I also have ²⁹seen thee, my son. Mayest thou prosper and fulfil the vow which thou hast vowed; and put not off thy vow; for thou shalt be called to account as touching the vow; now therefore make haste to perform it, and may He be pleased who has made all things, to whom thou hast vowed the vow.' ³⁰And he said to Rebecca: 'Go with Jacob thy son'; and Rebecca went with Jacob her son, and ³¹Deborah with her, and they came to Bethel. And Jacob remembered the prayer with which his father had blessed him and his two sons, Levi and Judah, and he rejoiced and blessed the God of his ³²fathers, Abraham and Isaac. And he said: 'Now I know that I have an eternal hope, and my sons also, before the God of all'; and thus is it ordained concerning the two; and they record it as an eternal testimony unto them on the heavenly tablets how Isaac blessed them.

Chapter 32

¹And he abode that night at Bethel, and Levi dreamed that they had ordained and made him the priest of the Most High God, him and his sons for ever; and he awoke from his sleep and blessed ²the Lord. And Jacob rose early in the morning, on the fourteenth of this month, and he gave a tithe of all that came with him, both of men and cattle, both of gold and every vessel and garment, ³yea, he gave tithes of all. And in those days Rachel became pregnant with her son Benjamin. And Jacob counted his sons from him upwards and Levi fell to the portion of the Lord, and his ⁴father clothed him in the garments of the priesthood and filled his hands. And on the fifteenth of this month, he brought to the altar fourteen oxen from amongst the cattle, and twenty-eight rams, and forty-nine sheep, and seven lambs, and twenty-one kids of the goats as a burnt-offering on the ⁵altar of sacrifice, well pleasing for a sweet savour before God. This was his offering, in consequence of the vow which he had vowed that he would give a tenth, with their fruit-offerings and their drink- ⁶offerings. And when the fire had consumed it, he burnt incense on the fire over the fire, and for a thank-offering two oxen and four rams and four sheep, four he-goats, and two sheep of a year old, ⁷and two kids of the goats; and thus he did daily for seven days. And he and all his sons and his men were eating this with joy there during seven days and blessing and thanking the Lord, who ⁸had delivered him out of all his tribulation and had given him his vow. And he tithed all the clean animals, and made a burnt sacrifice, but the unclean animals he gave not to Levi his son, and he ⁹gave him all the souls of the men And Levi discharged the priestly office at Bethel before Jacob

his father in preference to his ten brothers, and he was a priest there, and Jacob gave his vow: thus [10]he tithed again the tithe to the Lord and sanctified it, and it became holy unto Him. And for this reason it is ordained on the heavenly tablets as a law for the tithing again the tithe to eat before the Lord from year to year, in the place where it is chosen that His name should dwell, and to this law [11]there is no limit of days for ever. This ordinance is written that it may be fulfilled from year to year in eating the second tithe before the Lord in the place where it has been chosen, and nothing [12]shall remain over from it from this year to the year following. For in its year shall the seed be eaten till the days of the gathering of the seed of the year, and the wine till the days of the wine, [13]and the oil till the days of its season. And all that is left thereof and becomes old, let it be regarded [14]as polluted: let it be burnt with fire, for it is unclean. And thus let them eat it together in the [15]sanctuary, and let them not suffer it to become old. And all the tithes of the oxen and sheep shall be holy unto the Lord, and shall belong to his priests, which they will eat before Him from year to [16]year; for thus is it ordained and engraven regarding the tithe on the heavenly tablets. And on the following night, on the twenty-second day of this month, Jacob resolved to build that place, and to surround the court with a wall, and to sanctify it and make it holy for ever, for himself and his children [17]after him. And the Lord appeared to him by night and blessed him and said unto him: 'Thy name [18]shall not be called Jacob, but Israel shall they name thy name.' And He said unto him again: 'I am the Lord who created the heaven and the earth, and I will increase thee and multiply thee exceedingly, and kings shall come forth from thee, and they shall judge everywhere wherever the foot [19]of the sons of men has trodden. And I will give to thy seed all the earth which is under heaven, and they shall judge all the nations according to their desires, and after that they shall get possession [20]of the whole earth and inherit it for ever.' And He finished speaking with him, and He went up [21]from him. and Jacob looked till He had ascended into heaven. And he saw in a vision of the night, and behold an angel descended from heaven with seven tablets in his hands, and he gave them to Jacob, and he read them and knew all that was written therein which would befall him and his sons [21]throughout all the ages. And he showed him all that was written on the tablets, and said unto him: 'Do not build this place, and do not make it an eternal sanctuary, and do not dwell here; for this is not the place. Go to the house of Abraham thy father and dwell with Isaac thy father until the day [23]of the death of thy father. For in Egypt thou shalt die in peace, and in this land thou shalt be buried [24]with

The Book of Jubilees 81

honour in the sepulchre of thy fathers, with Abraham and Isaac. Fear not, for as thou hast seen and read it, thus shall it all be; and do thou write down everything as thou hast seen and read.' [25]And Jacob said: 'Lord, how can I remember all that I have read and seen 'And he said unto [26]him: 'I will bring all things to thy remembrance.' And he went up from him, and he awoke from his sleep, and he remembered everything which he had read and seen, and he wrote down all the [27]words which he had read and seen. And he celebrated there yet another day, and he sacrificed thereon according to all that he sacrificed on the former days, and called its name 'Addition,' for [28]this day was added and the former days he called 'The Feast '. And thus it was manifested that it should be, and it is written on the heavenly tablets: wherefore it was revealed to him that he should [29]celebrate it, and add it to the seven days of the feast. And its name was called 'Addition,' because that it was recorded amongst the days of the feast days, according to the number of [30]the days of the year. And in the night, on the twenty-third of this month, Deborah Rebecca's nurse died, and they buried her beneath the city under the oak of the river, and he called the name of this [31]place, 'The river of Deborah,' and the oak, 'The oak of the mourning of Deborah.' And Rebecca went and returned to her house to his father Isaac, and Jacob sent by her hand rams and sheep and [32]he-goats that she should prepare a meal for his father such as he desired. And he went after his [33]mother till he came to the land of Kabratan, and he dwelt there. And Rachel bare a son in the night, and called his name 'Son of my sorrow '; for she suffered in giving him birth: but his father called his name Benjamin, on the eleventh of the eighth month in the first of the sixth week of this [34]jubilee. And Rachel died there and she was buried in the land of Ephrath, the same is Bethlehem, and Jacob built a pillar on the grave of Rachel, on the road above her grave.

Chapter 33

[1]And Jacob went and dwelt to the south of Magdaladra'ef. And he went to his father Isaac, he [2]and Leah his wife, on the new moon of the tenth month. And Reuben saw Bilhah, Rachel's maid, [3]the concubine of his father, bathing in water in a secret place, and he loved her. And he hid himself at night, and he entered the house of Bilhah at night, and he found her sleeping alone on a bed in [4]her house. And he lay with her, and she awoke and saw, and behold Reuben was lying with her in the bed, and she uncovered the border of her covering and seized him, and cried out, and discovered [5]that it was Reuben. And she was ashamed because of him, and released her hand from him, and he [6],[7]fled. And she lamented because of

this thing exceedingly, and did not tell it to any one. And when Jacob returned and sought her, she said unto him: 'I am not clean for thee, for I have been defiled as regards thee; for Reuben has defiled me, and has lain with me in the night, and I was [8]asleep, and did not discover until he uncovered my skirt and slept with me.' And Jacob was exceedingly wroth with Reuben because he had lain with Bilhah, because he had uncovered his [9]father's skirt. And Jacob did not approach her again because Reuben had defiled her. And as for any man who uncovers his father's skirt his deed is wicked exceedingly, for he is abominable before [10]the Lord. For this reason it is written and ordained on the heavenly tablets that a man should not lie with his father's wife, and should not uncover his father's skirt, for this is unclean: they shall surely die together, the man who lies with his father's wife and the woman also, for they have [11]wrought uncleanness on the earth. And there shall be nothing unclean before our God in the nation [12]which He has chosen for Himself as a possession. And again, it is written a second time: 'Cursed be he who lieth with the wife of his father, for he hath uncovered his father's shame'; and all the [13]holy ones of the Lord said 'So be it; so be it.' And do thou, Moses, command the children of Israel that they observe this word; for it entails a punishment of death; and it is unclean, and there is no atonement for ever to atone for the man who has committed this, but he is to be put to death and slain, and stoned with stones, and rooted out from the midst of the people of our God. [14]For to no man who does so in Israel is it permitted to remain alive a single day on the earth, for he [15]is abominable and unclean. And let them not say: to Reuben was granted life and forgiveness after he had lain with his father's concubine, and to her also though she had a husband, and her husband [16]Jacob, his father, was still alive. For until that time there had not been revealed the ordinance and judgment and law in its completeness for all, but in thy days it has been revealed as a law of [17]seasons and of days, and an everlasting law for the everlasting generations. And for this law there is no consummation of days, and no atonement for it, but they must both be rooted out in the midst [18]of the nation: on the day whereon they committed it they shall slay them. And do thou, Moses, write it down for Israel that they may observe it, and do according to these words, and not commit a sin unto death; for the Lord our God is judge, who respects not persons and accepts not gifts. And tell them these words of the covenant, that they may hear and observe, and be on their guard with respect to them, and not be destroyed and rooted out of the land; for an uncleanness, and an abomination, and a contamination, and a pollution are all they who commit it on the earth before [20]our God. And there is no greater sin than the fornication which they commit on earth; for Israel is a holy nation unto the Lord its God, and a nation of inheritance, and a priestly and royal nation and for His own possession; and there shall no such uncleanness appear in the midst of the holy [21]nation. And in the third year of this sixth week Jacob and all his sons went and dwelt in the house [22]of Abraham, near Isaac his father and Rebecca his mother. And these were the names of the sons of Jacob: the first-born Reuben, Simeon, Levi, Judah, Issachar, Zebulon, the sons of Leah; and the sons of Rachel, Joseph and Benjamin; and the sons of Bilhah, Dan and Naphtali; and the sons of Zilpah, Gad and Asher; and Dinah, the daughter of Leah, the only daughter of Jacob. And they [23]came and bowed themselves to Isaac and Rebecca, and when they saw them they blessed Jacob and all his sons, and Isaac rejoiced exceedingly, for he saw the sons of Jacob, his younger son and he blessed them.

Chapter 34

[1]And in the sixth year of this week of this forty-fourth jubilee Jacob sent his sons to pasture their [2]sheep, and his servants with them to the pastures of Shechem. And the seven kings of the Amorites assembled themselves together against them, to slay them, hiding themselves under the trees, and [3]to take their cattle as a prey. And Jacob and Levi and Judah and Joseph were in the house with Isaac their father; for his spirit was sorrowful, and they could not leave him: and Benjamin was [4]the youngest, and for this reason remained with his father. And there came the kings of Taphu and the kings of 'Aresa, and the kings of Seragan, and the kings of Selo, and the kings of Ga'as, and the king of Bethoron, and the king of Ma'anisakir, and all those who dwell in these [5]mountains and who dwell in the woods in the land of Canaan. And they announced this to Jacob saying: 'Behold, the kings of the Amorites have surrounded thy sons, and plundered their herds.' [6]And he arose from his house, he and his three sons and all the servants of his father, and his own [7]servants, and he went against them with six thousand men, who carried swords. And he slew them in the pastures of Shechem, and pursued those who fled, and he slew them with the edge of the sword, and he slew 'Aresa and Taphu and Saregan and Selo and 'Amani-[8]sakir and Gaga'as, and he recovered his herds. And he prevailed over them, and imposed tribute on them that they should pay him tribute, five fruit products of their land, and he built Robel [9]and Tamnatares. And he returned in peace, and made peace with them, and they became his [10]servants, until the day that he and his sons went down into

Egypt. And in the seventh year of this week he sent Joseph to learn about the welfare of his brothers from his house to the land of Shechem, ¹¹and he found them in the land of Dothan. And they dealt treacherously with him, and formed a plot against him to slay him, but changing their minds, they sold him to Ishmaelite merchants, and they brought him down into Egypt, and they sold him to Potiphar, the eunuch of Pharaoh, the ¹²chief of the cooks, priest of the city of 'Elew. And the sons of Jacob slaughtered a kid, and dipped the coat of Joseph in the blood, and sent it to Jacob their father on the tenth of the seventh month. ¹³And he mourned all that night, for they had brought it to him in the evening, and he became feverish with mourning for his death, and he said: 'An evil beast hath devoured Joseph'; and all the members of his house mourned with him that day, and they were grieving and mourning with ¹⁴him all that day. And his sons and his daughter rose up to comfort him, but he refused to be ¹⁵comforted for his son. And on that day Bilhah heard that Joseph had perished, and she died mourning him, and she was living in Qafratef, and Dinah also, his daughter, died after Joseph had ¹⁶perished. And there came these three mournings upon Israel in one month. And they buried ¹⁷Bilhah over against the tomb of Rachel, and Dinah also. his daughter, they buried there. And he mourned for Joseph one year, and did not cease, for he said 'Let me go down to the grave mourning ¹⁸for my son'. For this reason it is ordained for the children of Israel that they should afflict themselves on the tenth of the seventh month -on the day that the news which made him weep for Joseph came to Jacob his father- that they should make atonement for themselves thereon with a young goat on the tenth of the seventh month, once a year, for their sins; for they had grieved the ¹⁹affection of their father regarding Joseph his son. And this day has been ordained that they should grieve thereon for their sins, and for all their transgressions and for all their errors, so that they ²⁰might cleanse themselves on that day once a year. And after Joseph perished, the sons of Jacob took unto themselves wives. The name of Reuben's wife is 'Ada; and the name of Simeon's wife is 'Adlba'a, a Canaanite; and the name of Levi's wife is Melka, of the daughters of Aram, of the seed of the sons of Terah; and the name of Judah's wife, Betasu'el, a Canaanite; and the name of Issachar's wife, Hezaqa: and the name of Zabulon's wife, Ni'iman; and the name of Dan's wife, 'Egla; and the name of Naphtali's wife, Rasu'u, of Mesopotamia; and the name of Gad's wife, Maka; and the name of Asher's wife, 'Ijona; and the name of Joseph's wife, Asenath, the Egyptian; and the name ²¹of Benjamin's wife, 'Ijasaka. And Simeon repented, and took a second wife from Mesopotamia as his brothers.

Chapter 35

¹And in the first year of the first week of the forty-fifth jubilee Rebecca called Jacob, her son, and commanded him regarding his father and regarding his brother, that he should honour them all the ²days of his life. And Jacob said: 'I will do everything as thou hast commanded me; for this thing will be honour and greatness to me, and righteousness before the Lord, that I should honour them. ³And thou too, mother, knowest from the time I was born until this day, all my deeds and all that is in ⁴my heart, that I always think good concerning all. And how should I not do this thing which thou ⁵hast commanded me, that I should honour my father and my brother! Tell me, mother, what ⁶perversity hast thou seen in me and I shall turn away from it, and mercy will be upon me.' And she said unto him: 'My son, I have not seen in thee all my days any perverse but only upright deeds. And yet I will tell thee the truth, my son: I shall die this year, and I shall not survive this year in my life; for I have seen in a dream the day of my death, that I should not live beyond a hundred and fifty-five years: and behold I have completed all the days of my life which I am to ⁷live.' And Jacob laughed at the words of his mother. because his mother had said unto him that she should die; and she was sitting opposite to him in possession of her strength, and she was not infirm in her strength; for she went in and out and saw, and her teeth were strong, and no ailment ⁸had touched her all the days of her life. And Jacob said unto her: 'Blessed am I, mother, if my days approach the days of thy life, and my strength remain with me thus as thy strength: and thou ⁹wilt not die, for thou art jesting idly with me regarding thy death.' And she went in to Isaac and said unto him: 'One petition I make unto thee: make Esau swear that he will not injure Jacob, nor pursue him with enmity; for thou knowest Esau's thoughts that they are perverse from his youth, ¹⁰and there is no goodness in him; for he desires after thy death to kill him. And thou knowest all that he has done since the day Jacob his brother went to Haran until this day: how he has forsaken us with his whole heart, and has done evil to us; thy flocks he has taken to himself, and carried off ¹¹all thy possessions from before thy face. And when we implored and besought him for what was ¹²our own, he did as a man who was taking pity on us. And he is bitter against thee because thou didst bless Jacob thy perfect and upright son; for there is no evil but only goodness in him, and since he came from Haran unto this day he has not robbed us of aught, for he brings us everything in its season always, and rejoices with all his heart when we take at his hands

and he blesses us, and has not parted from us since he came from Haran until this day, and he remains with us continually [13]at home honouring us.' And Isaac said unto her: 'I, too, know and see the deeds of Jacob who is with us, how that with all his heart he honours us; but I loved Esau formerly more than Jacob, because he was the firstborn; but now I love Jacob more than Esau, for he has done manifold evil deeds, and there is no righteousness in him, for all his ways are unrighteousness and violence, and [14]there is no righteousness around him. And now my heart is troubled because of all his deeds, and neither he nor his seed is to be saved, for they are those who will be destroyed from the earth and who will be rooted out from under heaven, for he has forsaken the God of Abraham and gone [15]after his wives and after their uncleanness and after their error, he and his children. And thou dost bid me make him swear that he will not slay Jacob his brother; even if he swear he will not abide [16]by his oath, and he will not do good but evil only. But if he desires to slay Jacob, his brother, into Jacob's hands will he be given, and he will not escape from his hands, for he will descend into his [17]hands. And fear thou not on account of Jacob; for the guardian of Jacob is great and powerful [18]and honoured, and praised more than the guardian of Esau.' And Rebecca sent and called Esau and he came to her, and she said unto him: 'I have a petition, my son, to make unto thee, and do [19]thou promise to do it, my son.' And he said: 'I will do everything that thou sayest unto me, and [20]I will not refuse thy petition.' And she said unto him: 'I ask you that the day I die, thou wilt take me in and bury me near Sarah, thy father's mother, and that thou and Jacob will love each other and that neither will desire evil against the other, but mutual love only, and so ye will prosper, my sons, and be honoured in the midst of the land, and no enemy will rejoice over you, and ye will be [21]a blessing and a mercy in the eyes of all those that love you.' And he said: 'I will do all that thou hast told me, and I shall bury thee on the day thou diest near Sarah, my father's mother, as [22]thou hast desired that her bones may be near thy bones. And Jacob, my brother, also, I shall love above all flesh; for I have not a brother in all the earth but him only: and this is no great merit for me if I love him; for he is my brother, and we were sown together in thy body, and together came [23]we forth from thy womb, and if I do not love my brother, whom shall I love And I, myself, beg thee to exhort Jacob concerning me and concerning my sons, for I know that he will assuredly be king over me and my sons, for on the day my father blessed him he made him the higher and me [24]the lower. And I swear unto thee that I shall love him, and not desire evil against him all the [25]days of my life but good only.' And he sware unto her regarding all this matter. And she called Jacob before the eyes of Esau, and gave him commandment according to the words which [26]she had spoken to Esau. And he said: 'I shall do thy pleasure; believe me that no evil will proceed from me or from my sons against Esau, and I shall be first in naught save in love only.' [27]And they eat and drank, she and her sons that night, and she died, three jubilees and one week and one year old, on that night, and her two sons, Esau and Jacob, buried her in the double cave near Sarah, their father's mother.

Chapter 36

[1]And in the sixth year of this week Isaac called his two sons Esau and Jacob, and they came to him, and he said unto them: 'My sons, I am going the way of my fathers, to the eternal house [2]where my fathers are. Wherefore bury me near Abraham my father, in the double cave in the field of Ephron the Hittite, where Abraham purchased a sepulchre to bury in; in the sepulchre which [3]I digged for myself, there bury me. And this I command you, my sons, that ye practise righteousness and uprightness on the earth, so that the Lord may bring upon you all that the Lord said that [4]he would do to Abraham and to his seed. And love one another, my sons, your brothers as a man who loves his own soul, and let each seek in what he may benefit his brother, and act together on the earth; and let them love each other as their own souls. And concerning the question of idols, I command and admonish you to reject them and hate them, and love them not, for they are full [6]of deception for those that worship them and for those that bow down to them. Remember ye, my sons, the Lord God of Abraham your father, and how I too worshipped Him and served Him in righteousness and in joy, that He might multiply you and increase your seed as the stars of heaven in multitude, and establish you on the earth as the plant of righteousness which will not be rooted [7]out unto all the generations for ever. And now I shall make you swear a great oath -for there is no oath which is greater than it by the name glorious and honoured and great and splendid and wonderful and mighty, which created the heavens and the earth and all things together- that ye will [8]fear Him and worship Him. And that each will love his brother with affection and righteousness, and that neither will desire evil against his brother from henceforth for ever all the days of your life [9]so that ye may prosper in all your deeds and not be destroyed. And if either of you devises evil against his brother, know that from henceforth everyone that devises evil against his brother shall fall into his hand, and shall be rooted out of the land of the living, and his seed shall be destroyed

from [10]under heaven. But on the day of turbulence and execration and indignation and anger, with flaming devouring fire as He burnt Sodom, so likewise will He burn his land and his city and all that is his, and he shall be blotted out of the book of the discipline of the children of men, and not be recorded in the book of life, but in that which is appointed to destruction, and he shall depart into eternal execration; so that their condemnation may be always renewed in hate and in execration and in wrath and in torment and in indignation and in plagues and in disease for ever. I say and testify to you, my sons, according to the judgment which shall come upon the man who wishes to [12]injure his brother. And he divided all his possessions between the two on that day and he gave the larger portion to him that was the first-born, and the tower and all that was about it, and all that [13]Abraham possessed at the Well of the Oath. And he said: 'This larger portion I will give to the [14]firstborn.' And Esau said, 'I have sold to Jacob and given my birthright to Jacob; to him let it be [15]given, and I have not a single word to say regarding it, for it is his.' And Isaac said, May a blessing rest upon you, my sons, and upon your seed this day, for ye have given me rest, and my heart is not [16]pained concerning the birthright, lest thou shouldest work wickedness on account of it. May the [17]Most High God bless the man that worketh righteousness, him and his seed for ever.' And he ended commanding them and blessing them, and they eat and drank together before him, and he rejoiced because there was one mind between them, and they went forth from him and rested that day and [18]slept. And Isaac slept on his bed that day rejoicing; and he slept the eternal sleep, and died one hundred and eighty years old. He completed twenty-five weeks and five years; and his two sons [19]Esau and Jacob buried him. And Esau went to the land of Edom, to the mountains of Seir, and [20]dwelt there. And Jacob dwelt in the mountains of Hebron, in the tower of the land of the sojournings of his father Abraham, and he worshipped the Lord with all his heart and according to the visible [21]commands according as He had divided the days of his generations. And Leah his wife died in the fourth year of the second week of the forty-fifth jubilee, and he buried her in the double cave [23]near Rebecca his mother to the left of the grave of Sarah, his father's mother and all her sons and his sons came to mourn over Leah his wife with him and to comfort him regarding her, for he [24]was lamenting her for he loved her exceedingly after Rachel her sister died; for she was perfect and upright in all her ways and honoured Jacob, and all the days that she lived with him he did not hear from her mouth a harsh word, for she was gentle and peaceable and upright and honourable ²⁴And he remembered all her deeds which she had done during her life and he lamented her exceedingly; for he loved her with all his heart and with all his soul.

Chapter 37

¹And on the day that Isaac the father of Jacob and Esau died, the sons of Esau heard that Isaac ²had given the portion of the elder to his younger son Jacob and they were very angry. And they strove with their father, saying 'Why has thy father given Jacob the portion of the elder and passed ³over thee, although thou art the elder and Jacob the younger' And he said unto them 'Because I sold my birthright to Jacob for a small mess of lentils, and on the day my father sent me to hunt and catch and bring him something that he should eat and bless me, he came with guile and brought ⁴my father food and drink, and my father blessed him and put me under his hand. And now our father has caused us to swear, me and him, that we shall not mutually devise evil, either against his brother, and that we shall continue in love and in peace each with his brother and not make our ways ⁵corrupt.' And they said unto him, 'We shall not hearken unto thee to make peace with him; for our strength is greater than his strength, and we are more powerful than he; we shall go against him and slay him, and destroy him and his sons. And if thou wilt not go with us, we shall do hurt ⁶to thee also. And now hearken unto us: Let us send to Aram and Philistia and Moab and Ammon, and let us choose for ourselves chosen men who are ardent for battle, and let us go against him and do battle with him, and let us exterminate him from the earth before he grows strong.' ⁷And their father said unto them, 'Do not go and do not make war with him lest ye fall before him.' ⁸And they said unto him, 'This too, is exactly thy mode of action from thy youth until this day, and ⁹thou art putting thy neck under his yoke. We shall not hearken to these words.' And they sent to Aram, and to 'Aduram to the friend of their father, and they hired along with them one thousand ¹⁰fighting men, chosen men of war. And there came to them from Moab and from the children of Ammon, those who were hired, one thousand chosen men, and from Philistia, one thousand chosen men of war, and from Edom and from the Horites one thousand chosen fighting men, and from the ¹¹Kittim mighty men of war. And they said unto their father: Go forth with them and lead them, ¹²else we shall slay thee.' And he was filled with wrath and indignation on seeing that his sons were forcing him to go before them to lead them against Jacob his brother. But afterward he remem- ¹³bered all the evil which lay hidden in his heart against Jacob his brother; and he remembered not the oath which he had sworn to his father and to his mother that he would devise

no evil all his days [14]against Jacob his brother. And notwithstanding all this, Jacob knew not that they were coming against him to battle, and he was mourning for Leah, his wife, until they approached very near to the [15]tower with four thousand warriors and chosen men of war And the men of Hebron sent to him saying, 'Behold thy brother has come against thee, to fight thee, with four thousand girt with the sword, and they carry shields and weapons'; for they loved Jacob more than Esau. So they told him; for [16]Jacob was a more liberal and merciful man than Esau. But Jacob would not believe until they came [17]very near to the tower. And he closed the gates of the tower; and he stood on the battlements and spake to his brother Esau and said, 'Noble is the comfort wherewith thou hast come to comfort me for my wife who has died. Is this the oath that thou didst swear to thy father and again to thy mother before they died Thou hast broken the oath, and on the moment that thou didst swear to [18]thy father wast thou condemned.' And then Esau answered and said unto him, 'Neither the children of men nor the beasts of the earth have any oath of righteousness which in swearing they have sworn an oath valid for ever; but every day they devise evil one against another, and how each [19]may slay his adversary and foe. And thou dost hate me and my children for ever. And there is [20]no observing the tie of brotherhood with thee. Hear these words which I declare unto thee, if the boar can change its skin and make its bristles as soft as wool, Or if it can cause horns to sprout forth on its head like the horns of a stag or of a sheep, Then will I observe the tie of brotherhood with thee And if the breasts separated themselves from their mother, for thou hast not been a brother to me. [21]And if the wolves make peace with the lambs so as not to devour or do them violence, And if their hearts are towards them for good, Then there shall be peace in my heart towards thee [22]and if the lion becomes the friend of the ox and makes peace with him And if he is bound under one yoke with him and ploughs with him, Then will I make peace with thee. [23]And when the raven becomes white as the raza, Then know that I have loved thee And shall make peace with thee Thou shalt be rooted out, And thy sons shall be rooted out, And there shall be no peace for thee' [24]and when Jacob saw that he was so evilly disposed towards him with his heart, and with all his soul as to slay him, and that he had come springing like the wild boar which comes upon [25]the spear that pierces and kills it, and recoils not from it; then he spake to his own and to his servants that they should attack him and all his companions.

Chapter 38

[1]And after that Judah spake to

Jacob, his father, and said unto him: 'Bend thy bow, father, and send forth thy arrows and cast down the adversary and slay the enemy; and mayst thou have the power, for we shall not slay thy brother, for he is such as thou, and he is like thee let us give him ²this honour.' Then Jacob bent his bow and sent forth the arrow and struck Esau, his brother on ³his right breast and slew him. And again he sent forth an arrow and struck 'Adoran the Aramaean, ⁴on the left breast, and drove him backward and slew him And then went forth the sons of Jacob, ⁵they and their servants, dividing themselves into companies on the four sides of the tower. And Judah went forth in front, and Naphtali and Gad with him and fifty servants with him on the south side of the tower, and they slew all they found before them, and not one individual of them escaped. ⁶And Levi and Dan and Asher went forth on the east side of the tower, and fifty men with them, ⁷and they slew the fighting men of Moab and Ammon. And Reuben and Issachar and Zebulon went forth on the north side of the tower, and fifty men with them, and they slew the fighting men of the ⁸Philistines. And Simeon and Benjamin and Enoch, Reuben's son, went forth on the west side of the tower, and fifty men with them, and they slew of Edom and of the Horites four hundred men, stout warriors; and six hundred fled, and four of the sons of Esau fled with them, and left their father ⁹lying slain, as he had fallen on the hill which is in 'Aduram. And the sons of Jacob pursued after them to the mountains of Seir. And Jacob buried his brother on the hill which is in 'Aduram, and ¹⁰he returned to his house. And the sons of Jacob pressed hard upon the sons of Esau in the moun- ¹¹tains of Seir, and bowed their necks so that they became servants of the sons of Jacob. And they ¹²sent to their father to inquire whether they should make peace with them or slay them. And Jacob sent word to his sons that they should make peace, and they made peace with them, and placed the ¹³yoke of servitude upon them, so that they paid tribute to Jacob and to his sons always. And they ¹⁴continued to pay tribute to Jacob until the day that he went down into Egypt. And the sons of Edom have not got quit of the yoke of servitude which the twelve sons of Jacob had imposed on ¹⁵them until this day. And these are the kings that reigned in Edom before there reigned any king ¹⁶over the children of Israel until this day in the land of Edom. And Balaq, the son of Beor, reigned ¹⁷in Edom, and the name of his city was Danaba. And Balaq died, and Jobab, the son of Zara of ¹⁸Boser, reigned in his stead. And Jobab died, and 'Asam, of the land of Teman, reigned in his stead. ¹⁹And 'Asam died, and 'Adath, the son of Barad, who slew Midian in the field of Moab, reigned in his ²⁰stead, and the name of his city was Avith. And 'Adath died, and Salman, from 'Amaseqa, reigned [21],[22]in his stead. And Salman died, and Saul of Ra'aboth by the river, reigned in his stead. And Saul [23]died, and Ba'elunan, the son of Achbor, reigned in his stead. And Ba'elunan, the son of Achbor died, and 'Adath reigned in his stead, and the name of his wife was Maitabith, the daughter of [25]Matarat, the daughter of Metabedza'ab. These are the kings who reigned in the land of Edom.

Chapter 39

[1],[2]And Jacob dwelt in the land of his father's sojournings in the land of Canaan. These are the generations of Jacob. And Joseph was seventeen years old when they took him down into [3]the land of Egypt, and Potiphar, an eunuch of Pharaoh, the chief cook bought him. And he set Joseph over all his house and the blessing of the Lord came upon the house of the Egyptian on [4]account of Joseph, and the Lord prospered him in all that he did. And the Egyptian committed everything into the hands of Joseph; for he saw that the Lord was with him, and that the [5]Lord prospered him in all that he did. And Joseph's appearance was comely and very beautiful was his appearance, and his master's wife lifted up her eyes and saw Joseph, and she loved him [6]and besought him to lie with her. But he did not surrender his soul, and he remembered the Lord and the words which Jacob, his father, used to read from amongst the words of Abraham, that no man should commit fornication with a woman who has a husband; that for him the punishment of death has been ordained in the heavens before the Most High God, and the sin [7]will be recorded against him in the eternal books continually before the Lord. And Joseph [8]remembered these words and refused to lie with her. And she besought him for a year, but he [9]refused and would not listen. But she embraced him and held him fast in the house in order to force him to lie with her, and closed the doors of the house and held him fast; but he left [10]his garment in her hands and broke through the door and fled without from her presence. And the woman saw that he would not lie with her, and she calumniated him in the presence of his lord, saying 'Thy Hebrew servant, whom thou lovest, sought to force me so that he might lie with me; and it came to pass when I lifted up my voice that he fled and left his garment in [11]my hands when I held him, and he brake through the door.' And the Egyptian saw the garment of Joseph and the broken door, and heard the words of his wife, and cast Joseph into [12]prison into the place where the prisoners were kept whom the king imprisoned. And he was there in the prison; and the Lord gave Joseph favour in the sight of the chief of the prison guards and compassion before him, for he saw that the Lord was

with him, and that the Lord [13]made all that he did to prosper. And he committed all things into his hands, and the chief of the prison guards knew of nothing that was with him, for Joseph did every thing, and the [14]Lord perfected it. And he remained there two years. And in those days Pharaoh, king of Egypt was wroth against his two eunuchs, against the chief butler, and against the chief baker, and he put [15]them in ward in the house of the chief cook, in the prison where Joseph was kept. And the chief of [16]the prison guards appointed Joseph to serve them; and he served before them. And they both [17]dreamed a dream, the chief butler and the chief baker, and they told it to Joseph. And as he interpreted to them so it befell them, and Pharaoh restored the chief butler to his office and the [18]chief baker he slew, as Joseph had interpreted to them. But the chief butler forgot Joseph in the prison, although he had informed him what would befall him, and did not remember to inform Pharaoh how Joseph had told him, for he forgot.

Chapter 40

[1]And in those days Pharaoh dreamed two dreams in one night concerning a famine which was to be in all the land, and he awoke from his sleep and called all the interpreters of dreams that were in Egypt, and magicians, and told them his two dreams, and they were not able to declare them. [2]And then the chief butler remembered Joseph and spake of him to the king, and he brought him [3]forth from the prison, and he told his two dreams before him. And he said before Pharaoh that his two dreams were one, and he said unto him: 'Seven years shall come in which there shall be plenty over all the land of Egypt, and after that seven years of famine, such a famine as has not been in all [4]the land. And now let Pharaoh appoint overseers in all the land of Egypt, and let them store up food in every city throughout the days of the years of plenty, and there will be food for the seven [5]years of famine, and the land will not perish through the famine, for it will be very severe.' And the Lord gave Joseph favour and mercy in the eyes of Pharaoh, and Pharaoh said unto his servants. We shall not find such a wise and discreet man as this man, for the spirit of the Lord is with [6]him.' And he appointed him the second in all his kingdom and gave him authority over all [7]Egypt, and caused him to ride in the second chariot of Pharaoh. And he clothed him with byssus garments, and he put a gold chain upon his neck, and a herald proclaimed before him ' 'El 'El wa 'Abirer,' and placed a ring on his hand and made him ruler over all his house, and magnified him, and [8]said unto him. 'Only on the throne shall I be greater than thou.' And Joseph ruled over all the land of Egypt, and all the princes of Pharaoh, and all his

servants, and all who did the king's business loved him, for he walked in uprightness, for he was without pride and arrogance, and he had no respect of persons, and did not accept gifts, but he judged in uprightness all the people of the land. ⁹And the land of Egypt was at peace before Pharaoh because of Joseph, for the Lord was with him, and gave him favour and mercy for all his generations before all those who knew him and those who heard concerning him, and Pharaoh's kingdom was well ordered, and there was no Satan and no evil ¹⁰person therein. And the king called Joseph's name Sephantiphans, and gave Joseph to wife the ¹¹daughter of Potiphar, the daughter of the priest of Heliopolis, the chief cook. And on the day that ¹²Joseph stood before Pharaoh he was thirty years old when he stood before Pharaoh. And in that year Isaac died. And it came to pass as Joseph had said in the interpretation of his two dreams, according as he had said it, there were seven years of plenty over all the land of Egypt, and the ¹³land of Egypt abundantly produced, one measure producing eighteen hundred measures. And Joseph gathered food into every city until they were full of corn until they could no longer count and measure it for its multitude.

Chapter 41

¹And in the forty-fifth jubilee, in the second week, and in the second year, Judah took for his ²first-born Er, a wife from the daughters of Aram, named Tamar. But he hated, and did not lie with her, because his mother was of the daughters of Canaan, and he wished to take him a wife of the ³kinsfolk of his mother, but Judah, his father, would not permit him. And this Er, the first-born of Judah, ⁴was wicked, and the Lord slew him. And Judah said unto Onan, his brother 'Go in unto thy brother's wife and perform the duty of a husband's brother unto her, and raise up seed unto thy brother.' And ⁵Onan knew that the seed would not be his, but his brother's only, and he went into the house of his brother's wife, and spilt the seed on the ground, and he was wicked in the eyes of the Lord, and He slew ⁶him. And Judah said unto Tamar, his daughter-in-law: 'Remain in thy father's house as a widow till ⁷Shelah my son be grown up, and I shall give thee to him to wife.' And he grew up; but Bedsu'el, the wife of Judah, did not permit her son Shelah to marry. And Bedsu'el, the wife of Judah, died ⁸in the fifth year of this week. And in the sixth year Judah went up to shear his sheep at Timnah. ⁹And they told Tamar: 'Behold thy father-in-law goeth up to Timnah to shear his sheep.' And she put off her widow's clothes, and put on a veil, and adorned herself, and sat in the gate adjoining the ¹⁰way to Timnah. And as Judah was going along he found her, and thought her to be an harlot, and he said unto her: 'Let me

come in unto thee'; and she said unto him Come in,' and he went ¹¹in. And she said unto him: 'Give me my hire'; and he said unto her: 'I have nothing in my ¹²hand save my ring that is on my finger, and my necklace, and my staff which is in my hand.' And she said unto him 'Give them to me until thou dost send me my hire', and he said unto her: 'I will send unto thee a kid of the goats'; and he gave them to her, , and ¹³,¹⁴she conceived by him. And Judah went unto his sheep, and she went to her father's house. And Judah sent a kid of the goats by the hand of his shepherd, an Adullamite, and he found her not; and he asked the people of the place, saying: 'Where is the harlot who was here' And they said ¹⁵unto him; 'There is no harlot here with us.' And he returned and informed him, and said unto him that he had not found her: 'I asked the people of the place, and they said unto me: "There ¹⁶is no harlot here." ' And he said: 'Let her keep them lest we become a cause of derision.' And when she had completed three months, it was manifest that she was with child, and they told Judah, ¹⁷saying: 'Behold Tamar, thy daughter-in-law, is with child by whoredom.' And Judah went to the house of her father, and said unto her father and her brothers: 'Bring her forth, and let them burn ¹⁸her, for she hath wrought uncleanness in Israel.' And it came to pass when they brought her forth to burn her that she sent to her father-in-law the ring and the necklace, and the staff, saying: ¹⁹'Discern whose are these, for by him am I with child.' And Judah acknowledged, and said: 'Tamar ²⁰is more righteous than I am. And therefore let them burn her not' And for that reason she was ²¹not given to Shelah, and he did not again approach her And after that she bare two sons, Perez ²²and Zerah, in the seventh year of this second week. And thereupon the seven years of fruitfulness ²³were accomplished, of which Joseph spake to Pharaoh. And Judah acknowledged that the deed which he had done was evil, for he had lain with his daughter-in-law, and he esteemed it hateful in his eyes, and he acknowledged that he had transgressed and gone astray, for he had uncovered the skirt of his son, and he began to lament and to supplicate before the Lord because of his transgression. ²⁴And we told him in a dream that it was forgiven him because he supplicated earnestly, and lamented, ²⁵and did not again commit it. And he received forgiveness because he turned from his sin and from his ignorance, for he transgressed greatly before our God; and every one that acts thus, every one who lies with his mother-in-law, let them burn him with fire that he may burn therein, for there is ²⁶uncleanness and pollution upon them, with fire let them burn them. And do thou command the children of Israel that there be no uncleanness amongst them, for every one who lies with his daughter-in-law or with his mother-in-law hath wrought uncleanness; with fire let them burn the man who has lain with her, and likewise the woman, and He will turn away wrath and punishment [27] from Israel. And unto Judah we said that his two sons had not lain with her, and for this reason [28] his seed was stablished for a second generation, and would not be rooted out. For in singleness of eye he had gone and sought for punishment, namely, according to the judgment of Abraham, which he had commanded his sons, Judah had sought to burn her with fire.

Chapter 42

[1] And in the first year of the third week of the forty-fifth jubilee the famine began to come into the [2] land, and the rain refused to be given to the earth, for none whatever fell. And the earth grew barren, but in the land of Egypt there was food, for Joseph had gathered the seed of the land in the [3] seven years of plenty and had preserved it. And the Egyptians came to Joseph that he might give them food, and he opened the store-houses where was the grain of the first year, and he sold it to [4] the people of the land for gold. , and Jacob heard that there was food in Egypt, and he sent his ten sons that they should procure food for him in Egypt; but Benjamin he did not send, and arrived among those [5] that went there. And Joseph recognised them, but they did not recognise him, and he spake unto them and questioned them, and he said unto them; 'Are ye not spies and have ye not come to [6] explore the approaches of the land 'And he put them in ward. And after that he set them free [7] again, and detained Simeon alone and sent off his nine brothers. And he filled their sacks with corn, [8] and he put their gold in their sacks, and they did not know. And he commanded them to bring [9] their younger brother, for they had told him their father was living and their younger brother. And they went up from the land of Egypt and they came to the land of Canaan; and they told their father all that had befallen them, and how the lord of the country had spoken roughly to them, and [10] had seized Simeon till they should bring Benjamin. And Jacob said: 'Me have ye bereaved of my children! Joseph is not and Simeon also is not, and ye will take Benjamin away. On me has your [11] wickedness come. 'And he said: 'My son will not go down with you lest perchance he fall sick; for their mother gave birth to two sons, and one has perished, and this one also ye will take from me. If perchance he took a fever on the road, ye would bring down my old age with sorrow unto death.' [12] For he saw that their money had been returned to every man in his sack, and for this reason he [13] feared to send him. And

the famine increased and became sore in the land of Canaan, and in all lands save in the land of Egypt, for many of the children of the Egyptians had stored up their seed for food from the time when they saw Joseph gathering seed together and putting it in storehouses [14]and preserving it for the years of famine. And the people of Egypt fed themselves thereon during [15]the first year of their famine But when Israel saw that the famine was very sore in the land, and that there was no deliverance, he said unto his sons: 'Go again, and procure food for us that we die [16]not.' And they said: 'We shall not go; unless our youngest brother go with us, we shall not go.' [17]And Israel saw that if he did not send him with them, they should all perish by reason of the famine [18]And Reuben said: 'Give him into my hand, and if I do not bring him back to thee, slay my two [19]sons instead of his soul.' And he said unto him: 'He shall not go with thee.' And Judah came near and said: 'Send him with me, and if I do not bring him back to thee, let me bear the blame before [20]thee all the days of my life.' And he sent him with them in the second year of this week on the first day of the month, and they came to the land of Egypt with all those who went, and they had [21]presents in their hands, stacte and almonds and terebinth nuts and pure honey. And they went and stood before Joseph, and he saw Benjamin his brother, and he knew him, and said unto them: Is this your youngest brother' And they said unto him: 'It is he.' And he said The Lord be [22]gracious to thee, my son!' And he sent him into his house and he brought forth Simeon unto them and he made a feast for them, and they presented to him the gift which they had brought in their [23]hands. And they eat before him and he gave them all a portion, but the portion of Benjamin was [24]seven times larger than that of any of theirs. And they eat and drank and arose and remained with [25]their asses. And Joseph devised a plan whereby he might learn their thoughts as to whether thoughts of peace prevailed amongst them, and he said to the steward who was over his house: 'Fill all their sacks with food, and return their money unto them into their vessels, and my cup, the silver cup out of which I drink, put it in the sack of the youngest, and send them away.'

Chapter 43

[1]And he did as Joseph had told him, and filled all their sacks for them with food and put their [2]money in their sacks, and put the cup in Benjamin's sack. Aud early in the morning they departed, and it came to pass that, when they had gone from thence, Joseph said unto the steward of his house: 'Pursue them, run and seize them, saying, "For good ye have requited me with evil; you have stolen from me the silver cup out of which my lord drinks." And bring back to me

their ³youngest brother, and fetch him quickly before I go forth to my seat of judgment.' And he ran ⁴after them and said unto them according to these words. And they said unto him: 'God forbid that thy servants should do this thing, and steal from the house of thy lord any utensil, and the money also which we found in our sacks the first time, we thy servants brought back from the land of ⁵Canaan. How then should we steal any utensil Behold here are we and our sacks search, and wherever thou findest the cup in the sack of any man amongst us, let him be slain, and we and our ⁶asses will serve thy lord.' And he said unto them: 'Not so, the man with whom I find, him only ⁷shall I take as a servant, and ye shall return in peace unto your house.' And as he was searching in their vessels, beginning with the eldest and ending with the youngest, it was found in Benjamin's ⁸sack. And they rent their garments, and laded their asses, and returned to the city and came to the ⁹house of Joseph, and they all bowed themselves on their faces to the ground before him. And Joseph said unto them: 'Ye have done evil.' And they said: 'What shall we say and how shall we defend ourselves Our lord hath discovered the transgression of his servants; behold we are the ¹⁰servants of our lord, and our asses also. 'And Joseph said unto them: 'I too fear the Lord; as for you, go ye to your homes and let your brother be my servant, for ye have done evil. Know ye not ¹¹that a man delights in his cup as I with this cup And yet ye have stolen it from me.' And Judah said: 'O my lord, let thy servant, I pray thee, speak a word in my lord's ear two brothers did thy servant's mother bear to our father: one went away and was lost, and hath not been found, and he alone is left of his mother, and thy servant our father loves him, and his life also is bound up with ¹²the life of this lad. And it will come to pass, when we go to thy servant our father, and the lad is ¹³not with us, that he will die, and we shall bring down our father with sorrow unto death. Now rather let me, thy servant, abide instead of the boy as a bondsman unto my lord, and let the lad go with his brethren, for I became surety for him at the hand of thy servant our father, and if I do not ¹⁴bring him back, thy servant will hear the blame to our father for ever.' And Joseph saw that they were all accordant in goodness one with another, and he could not refrain himself, and he told them ¹⁵that he was Joseph. And he conversed with them in the Hebrew tongue and fell on their neck and ¹⁶wept. But they knew him not and they began to weep. And he said unto them: 'Weep not over me, but hasten and bring my father to me; and ye see that it is my mouth that speaketh and the ¹⁷eyes of my brother Benjamin see. For behold this is the second year of the famine, and there are ¹⁸still five years without harvest or fruit of trees or ploughing. Come down quickly ye and your households, so that ye perish not through the famine, and do not be grieved for your possessions, for [19]the Lord sent me before you to set things in order that many people might live. And tell my father that I am still alive, and ye, behold, ye see that the Lord has made me as a father to Pharaoh, [20]and ruler over his house and over all the land of Egypt. And tell my father of all my glory, and [21]all the riches and glory that the Lord hath given me.' And by the command of the mouth of Pharaoh he gave them chariots and provisions for the way, and he gave them all many-coloured [21]raiment and silver. And to their father he sent raiment and silver and ten asses which carried corn, [23]and he sent them away. And they went up and told their father that Joseph was alive, and was measuring out corn to all the nations of the earth, and that he was ruler over all the land of Egypt. [24]And their father did not believe it, for he was beside himself in his mind; but when he saw the wagons which Joseph had sent, the life of his spirit revived, and he said: 'It is enough for me if Joseph lives; I will go down and see him before I die.'

Chapter 44

[1]And Israel took his journey from Haran from his house on the new moon of the third month, and he went on the way of the Well of the Oath, and he offered a sacrifice to the God of his [2]father Isaac on the seventh of this month. And Jacob remembered the dream that he had seen [3]at Bethel, and he feared to go down into Egypt. And while he was thinking of sending word to Joseph to come to him, and that he would not go down, he remained there seven days, if [4]perchance he could see a vision as to whether he should remain or go down. And he celebrated the harvest festival of the first-fruits with old grain, for in all the land of Canaan there was not a handful of seed in the land, for the famine was over all the beasts and cattle and [5]birds, and also over man. And on the sixteenth the Lord appeared unto him, and said unto him, 'Jacob, Jacob'; and he said, 'Here am I.' And He said unto him: 'I am the God of thy fathers, the God of Abraham and Isaac; fear not to go down into Egypt, for I will there make of thee [6]a great nation I will go down with thee, and I will bring thee up again, and in this land shalt thou be buried, and Joseph shall put his hands upon thy eyes. Fear not; go down into Egypt.' [7]And his sons rose up, and his sons' sons, and they placed their father and their possessions upon [8]wagons. And Israel rose up from the Well of the Oath on the sixteenth of this third month, and he [9]went to the land of Egypt. And Israel sent Judah before him to his son Joseph to examine the Land of Goshen, for Joseph had told his brothers that they should come and dwell there that they

[10]might be near him. And this was the goodliest land in the land of Egypt, and near to him, for all [11]of them and also for the cattle. And these are the names of the sons of Jacob who went into [12]Egypt with Jacob their father Reuben, the First-born of Israel; and these are the names of his [13]sons Enoch, and Pallu, and Hezron and Carmi-five. Simeon and his sons; and these are the names of his sons: Jemuel, and Jamin, and Ohad, and Jachin, and Zohar, and Shaul, the son [14]of the Zephathite woman-seven. Levi and his sons; and these are the names of his sons: Gershon, and Kohath, and Merari-four. Judah and his sons; and these are the names of his sons: [15]Shela, and Perez, and Zerah-four. Issachar and his sons; and these are the names of his sons: [17]Tola, and Phua, and Jasub, and Shimron-five. Zebulon and his sons; and these are the names of [18]his sons: Sered, and Elon, and Jahleel-four. And these are the sons of Jacob and their sons whom Leah bore to Jacob in Mesopotamia, six, and their one sister, Dinah and all the souls of the sons of Leah, and their sons, who went with Jacob their father into Egypt, were twenty-nine, and Jacob their [19]father being with them, they were thirty. And the sons of Zilpah, Leah's handmaid, the wife of [20]Jacob, who bore unto Jacob Gad and Ashur. And there are the names of their sons who went with him into Egypt. The sons of Gad: Ziphion, and Haggi, and Shuni, and Ezbon, and Eri, and Areli, [21]and Arodi-eight. And the sons of Asher: Imnah, and Ishvah, and Ishvi, and Beriah, and Serah, [22],[23]their one sister-six. All the souls were fourteen, and all those of Leah were forty-four. And the [24]sons of Rachel, the wife of Jacob: Joseph and Benjamin. And there were born to Joseph in Egypt before his father came into Egypt, those whom Asenath, daughter of Potiphar priest of Heliopolis [25]bare unto him, Manasseh, and Ephraim-three. And the sons of Benjamin: Bela and Becher and Ashbel, Gera, and Naaman, and Ehi, and Rosh, and Muppim, and Huppim, and Ard-eleven. [26],[27]And all the souls of Rachel were fourteen. And the sons of Bilhah, the handmaid of Rachel, the [28]wife of Jacob, whom she bare to Jacob, were Dan and Naphtali. And these are the names of their sons who went with them into Egypt. And the sons of Dan were Hushim, and Samon, and Asudi. [29]and 'Ijaka, and Salomon-six. And they died the year in which they entered into Egypt, and there [30]was left to Dan Hushim alone. And these are the names of the sons of Naphtali Jahziel, and Guni [31]and Jezer, and Shallum, and 'Iv. And 'Iv, who was born after the years of famine, died in Egypt. [32],[33]And all the souls of Rachel were twenty-six. And all the souls of Jacob which went into Egypt were seventy souls. These are his children and his children's children, in all seventy, but five died [34]in Egypt before Joseph, and

had no children. And in the land of Canaan two sons of Judah died, Er and Onan, and they had no children, and the children of Israel buried those who perished, and they were reckoned among the seventy Gentile nations.

Chapter 45

¹And Israel went into the country of Egypt, into the land of Goshen, on the new moon of the fourth. ²month, in the second year of the third week of the forty-fifth jubilee. And Joseph went to meet his ³father Jacob, to the land of Goshen, and he fell on his father's neck and wept. And Israel said unto Joseph: 'Now let me die since I have seen thee, and now may the Lord God of Israel be blessed the God of Abraham and the God of Isaac who hath not withheld His mercy and His grace from ⁴His servant Jacob. It is enough for me that I have seen thy face whilst I am yet alive; yea, true is the vision which I saw at Bethel. Blessed be the Lord my God for ever and ever, and blessed be ⁵His name.' And Joseph and his brothers eat bread before their father and drank wine, and Jacob rejoiced with exceeding great joy because he saw Joseph eating with his brothers and drinking before him, and he blessed the Creator of all things who had preserved him, and had preserved for him his ⁶twelve sons. And Joseph had given to his father and to his brothers as a gift the right of dwelling in the land of Goshen and in Rameses and all the region round about, which he ruled over before Pharaoh. And Israel and his sons dwelt in the land of Goshen, the best part of the land of Egypt ⁷and Israel was one hundred and thirty years old when he came into Egypt. And Joseph nourished his father and his brethren and also their possessions with bread as much as sufficed them for the ⁸seven years of the famine. And the land of Egypt suffered by reason of the famine, and Joseph acquired all the land of Egypt for Pharaoh in return for food, and he got possession of the people ⁹and their cattle and everything for Pharaoh. And the years of the famine were accomplished, and Joseph gave to the people in the land seed and food that they might sow the land in the eighth ¹⁰year, for the river had overflowed all the land of Egypt. For in the seven years of the famine it had not overflowed and had irrigated only a few places on the banks of the river, but now it overflowed ¹¹and the Egyptians sowed the land, and it bore much corn that year. And this was the first year of ¹²the fourth week of the forty-fifth jubilee. And Joseph took of the corn of the harvest the fifth part for the king and left four parts for them for food and for seed, and Joseph made it an ordinance for ¹³the land of Egypt until this day. And Israel lived in the land of Egypt seventeen years, and all the days which he lived were three jubilees, one hundred and forty-seven years, and he died in the

fourth ¹⁴year of the fifth week of the forty-fifth jubilee. And Israel blessed his sons before he died and told them everything that would befall them in the land of Egypt; and he made known to them what would come upon them in the last days, and blessed them and gave to Joseph two portions in ¹⁵the land. And he slept with his fathers, and he was buried in the double cave in the land of Canaan, near Abraham his father in the grave which he dug for himself in the double cave in ¹⁶the land of Hebron. And he gave all his books and the books of his fathers to Levi his son that he might preserve them and renew them for his children until this day.

Chapter 46

¹And it came to pass that after Jacob died the children of Israel multiplied in the land of Egypt, and they became a great nation, and they were of one accord in heart, so that brother loved brother and every man helped his brother, and they increased abundantly and multiplied exceedingly, ten ²weeks of years, all the days of the life of Joseph And there was no Satan nor any evil all the days of the life of Joseph which he lived after his father Jacob, for all the Egyptians honoured the children ³of Israel all the days of the life of Joseph. And Joseph died being a hundred and ten years old; seventeen years he lived in the land of Canaan, and ten years he was a servant, and three years in ⁴prison, and eighty years he was under the king, ruling all the land of Egypt. And he died and all ⁵his brethren and all that generation. And he commanded the children of Israel before he died that ⁶they should carry his bones with them when they went forth from the land of Egypt. And he made them swear regarding his bones, for he knew that the Egyptians would not again bring forth and bury him in the land of Canaan, for Makamaron, king of Canaan, while dwelling in the land of Assyria, fought in the valley with the king of Egypt and slew him there, and pursued after the ⁷Egyptians to the gates of 'Ermon. But he was not able to enter, for another, a new king, had become king of Egypt, and he was stronger than he, and he returned to the land of Canaan, and the gates of ⁸Egypt were closed, and none went out and none came into Egypt. And Joseph died in the forty-sixth jubilee, in the sixth week, in the second year, and they buried him in the land of Egypt, and ⁹all his brethren died after him. And the king of Egypt went forth to war with the king of Canaan in the forty-seventh jubilee, in the second week in the second year, and the children of Israel brought forth all the bones of the children of Jacob save the bones of Joseph, and they buried them in the ¹⁰field in the double cave in the mountain. And the most of them returned to Egypt, but a few of ¹¹them remained in the mountains of Hebron,

and Amram thy father remained with them. And the [12]king of Canaan was victorious over the king of Egypt, and he closed the gates of Egypt. And he devised an evil device against the children of Israel of afflicting them and he said unto the people of [13]Egypt: 'Behold the people of the children of Israel have increased and multiplied more than we. Come and let us deal wisely with them before they become too many, and let us afflict them with slavery before war come upon us and before they too fight against us; else they will join themselves unto our enemies and get them up out of our land, for their hearts and faces are towards the land [14]of Canaan.' And he set over them taskmasters to afflict them with slavery; and they built strong cities for Pharaoh, Pithom, and Raamses and they built all the walls and all the fortifications which [15]had fallen in the cities of Egypt. And they made them serve with rigour, and the more they dealt evilly with them, the more they increased and multiplied. And the people of Egypt abominated the children of Israel

Chapter 47

[1]And in the seventh week, in the seventh year, in the forty-seventh jubilee, thy father went forth from the land of Canaan, and thou wast born in the fourth week, in the sixth year thereof, in the [2]forty-eighth jubilee; this was the time of tribulation on the children of Israel. And Pharaoh, king of Egypt, issued a command regarding them that they should cast all their male children which were [3]born into the river. And they cast them in for seven months until the day that thou wast born [4]And thy mother hid thee for three months, and they told regarding her. And she made an ark for thee, and covered it with pitch and asphalt, and placed it in the flags on the bank of the river, and she placed thee in it seven days, and thy mother came by night and suckled thee, and by day [5]Miriam, thy sister, guarded thee from the birds. And in those days Tharmuth, the daughter of Pharaoh, came to bathe in the river, and she heard thy voice crying, and she told her maidens to [6]bring thee forth, and they brought thee unto her. And she took thee out of the ark, and she had [7]compassion on thee. And thy sister said unto her: 'Shall I go and call unto thee one of the [8]Hebrew women to nurse and suckle this babe for thee' And she said unto her: 'Go.' And she [9]went and called thy mother Jochebed, and she gave her wages, and she nursed thee. And afterwards, when thou wast grown up, they brought thee unto the daughter of Pharaoh, and thou didst become her son, and Amram thy father taught thee writing, and after thou hadst completed three weeks [10]they brought thee into the royal court. And thou wast three weeks of years at court until the time when thou didst go forth from the royal court and didst see an Egyptian

smiting thy friend who was [11]of the children of Israel, and thou didst slay him and hide him in the sand. And on the second day thou didst and two of the children of Israel striving together, and thou didst say to him who was [12]doing the wrong: 'Why dost thou smite thy brother' And he was angry and indignant, and said: 'Who made thee a prince and a judge over us Thinkest thou to kill me as thou killedst the Egyptian yesterday' And thou didst fear and flee on account of these words.

Chapter 48

[1]And in the sixth year of the third week of the forty-ninth jubilee thou didst depart and dwell in the land of Midian, five weeks and one year. And thou didst return into Egypt in the second week [2]in the second year in the fiftieth jubilee. And thou thyself knowest what He spake unto thee on Mount Sinai, and what prince Mastema desired to do with thee when thou wast returning into Egypt [3]. Did he not with all his power seek to slay thee and deliver the Egyptians out of thy hand when he saw that thou wast sent to execute [4]judgment and vengeance on the Egyptians And I delivered thee out of his hand, and thou didst perform the signs and wonders which thou wast sent to perform in Egypt against Pharaoh, and [5]against all his house, and against his servants and his people. And the Lord executed a great vengeance on them for Israel's sake, and smote them through the plagues of blood and frogs, lice and dog-flies, and malignant boils breaking forth in blains; and their cattle by death; and by hail-stones, thereby He destroyed everything that grew for them; and by locusts which devoured the residue which had been left by the hail, and by darkness; and by the death of the first-born of [6]men and animals, and on all their idols the Lord took vengeance and burned them with fire And everything was sent through thy hand, that thou shouldst declare these things before they were done, and thou didst speak with the king of Egypt before all his servants and before his people [7]And everything took place according to thy words; ten great and terrible judgments came on the [8]land of Egypt that thou mightest execute vengeance on it for Israel. And the Lord did everything for Israel's sake, and according to His covenant, which he had ordained with Abraham that He [9]would take vengeance on them as they had brought them by force into bondage. And the prince Mastema stood up against thee, and sought to cast thee into the hands of Pharaoh, and he helped [10]the Egyptian sorcerers, and they stood up and wrought before thee the evils indeed we permitted [11]them to work, but the remedies we did not allow to be wrought by their hands. And the Lord smote them with malignant ulcers, and they were not able to stand, for we

destroyed them so that [12]they could not perform a single sign. And notwithstanding all these signs and wonders the prince Mastema was not put to shame because he took courage and cried to the Egyptians to pursue after thee with all the powers of the Egyptians, with their chariots, and with their horses, and with all the [13]hosts of the peoples of Egypt. And I stood between the Egyptians and Israel, and we delivered Israel out of his hand, and out of the hand of his people, and the Lord brought them through the [14]midst of the sea as if it were dry land. And all the peoples whom he brought to pursue after Israel, the Lord our God cast them into the midst of the sea, into the depths of the abyss beneath the children of Israel, even as the people of Egypt had cast their children into the river He took vengeance on [1],000,000of them, and one thousand strong and energetic men were destroyed on [15]account of one suckling of the children of thy people which they had thrown into the river. And on the fourteenth day and on the fifteenth and on the sixteenth and on the seventeenth and on the eighteenth the prince Mastema was bound and imprisoned behind the children of Israel that he [16]might not accuse them. And on the nineteenth we let them loose that they might help the [17]Egyptians and pursue the children of Israel. And he hardened their hearts and made them stubborn, and the device was devised by the Lord our God that He might smite the Egyptians and [18]cast them into the sea. And on the fourteenth we bound him that he might not accuse the children of Israel on the day when they asked the Egyptians for vessels and garments, vessels of silver, and vessels of gold, and vessels of bronze, in order to despoil the Egyptians in return for the bondage in [19]which they had forced them to serve. And we did not lead forth the children of Israel from Egypt empty handed.

Chapter 49

[1]Remember the commandment which the Lord commanded thee concerning the passover, that thou shouldst celebrate it in its season on the fourteenth of the first month, that thou shouldst kill it before it is evening, and that they should eat it by night on the evening of the fifteenth from the [2]time of the setting of the sun. For on this night -the beginning of the festival and the beginning of the joy- ye were eating the passover in Egypt, when all the powers of Mastema had been let loose to slay all the first-born in the land of Egypt, from the first-born of Pharaoh to the first-born [3]of the captive maid-servant in the mill, and to the cattle. And this is the sign which the Lord gave them: Into every house on the lintels of which they saw the blood of a lamb of the first year, into that house they should not enter to slay, but should

pass by it, that all those should be saved that ⁴were in the house because the sign of the blood was on its lintels. And the powers of the Lord did everything according as the Lord commanded them, and they passed by all the children of Israel, and the plague came not upon them to destroy from amongst them any soul either of cattle, or ⁵man, or dog. And the plague was very grievous in Egypt, and there was no house in Egypt ⁶where there was not one dead, and weeping and lamentation. And all Israel was eating the flesh of the paschal lamb, and drinking the wine, and was lauding, and blessing, and giving thanks to the Lord God of their fathers, and was ready to go forth from under the yoke of Egypt, and from ⁷the evil bondage. And remember thou this day all the days of thy life, and observe it from year to year all the days of thy life, once a year, on its day, according to all the law thereof, and do not ⁸adjourn it from day to day, or from month to month. For it is an eternal ordinance, and engraven on the heavenly tablets regarding all the children of Israel that they should observe it every year on its day once a year, throughout all their generations; and there is no limit of days, for this is ordained ⁹for ever. And the man who is free from uncleanness, and does not come to observe it on occasion of its day, so as to bring an acceptable offering before the Lord, and to eat and to drink before the Lord on the day of its festival, that man who is clean and close at hand shall be cut off: because he offered not the oblation of the Lord in its appointed season, he shall take the guilt upon himself. ¹⁰Let the children of Israel come and observe the passover on the day of its fixed time, on the fourteenth day of the first month, between the evenings, from the third part of the day to the third part of ¹the night, for two portions of the day are given to the light, and a third part to the evening. This ¹²is that which the Lord commanded thee that thou shouldst observe it between the evenings. And it is not permissible to slay it during any period of the light, but during the period bordering on the evening, and let them eat it at the time of the evening, until the third part of the night, and whatever is left over of all its flesh from the third part of the night and onwards, let them burn ¹³it with fire. And they shall not cook it with water, nor shall they eat it raw, but roast on the fire: they shall eat it with diligence, its head with the inwards thereof and its feet they shall roast with fire, and not break any bone thereof; for of the children of Israel no bone shall be crushed. ¹⁴For this reason the Lord commanded the children of Israel to observe the passover on the day of its fixed time, and they shall not break a bone thereof; for it is a festival day, and a day commanded, and there may be no passing over from day to day, and month to month, but on the day of its [15]festival let it be observed. And do thou command the children of Israel to observe the passover throughout their days, every year, once a year on the day of its fixed time, and it shall come for a memorial well pleasing before the Lord, and no plague shall come upon them to slay or to smite in that year in which they celebrate the passover in its season in every respect according to His [16]command. And they shall not eat it outside the sanctuary of the Lord, but before the sanctuary of the Lord, and all the people of the congregation of Israel shall celebrate it in its appointed season. [17]And every man who has come upon its day shall eat it in the sanctuary of your God before the Lord from twenty years old and upward; for thus is it written and ordained that they should eat it [18]in the sanctuary of the Lord. And when the children of Israel come into the land which they are to possess, into the land of Canaan, and set up the tabernacle of the Lord in the midst of the land in one of their tribes until the sanctuary of the Lord has been built in the land, let them come and celebrate the passover in the midst of the tabernacle of the Lord, and let them slay it [19]before the Lord from year to year. And in the days when the house has been built in the name of the Lord in the land of their inheritance, they shall go there and slay the passover in the evening, at [20]sunset, at the third part of the day. And they shall offer its blood on the threshold of the altar, and shall place its fat on the fire which is upon the altar, and they shall eat its flesh roasted [21]with fire in the court of the house which has been sanctified in the name of the Lord. And they may not celebrate the passover in their cities, nor in any place save before the tabernacle of the Lord, or before His house where His name hath dwelt; and they shall not go astray from the Lord. [22]And do thou, Moses, command the children of Israel to observe the ordinances of the passover, as it was commanded unto thee; declare thou unto them every year and the day of its days, and the festival of unleavened bread, that they should eat unleavened bread seven days, and that they should observe its festival, and that they bring an oblation every day during those seven days of [23]joy before the Lord on the altar of your God. For ye celebrated this festival with haste when ye went forth from Egypt till ye entered into the wilderness of Shur; for on the shore of the sea ye completed it.

Chapter 50

[1]And after this law I made known to thee the days of the Sabbaths in the desert of Sinai, which [2]is between Elim and Sinai. And I told thee of the Sabbaths of the land on Mount Sinai, and I told thee of the jubilee years in the sabbaths of years: but the year thereof have I not told thee till ye

³enter the land which ye are to possess. And the land also shall keep its sabbaths while they dwell ⁴upon it, and they shall know the jubilee year. Wherefore I have ordained for thee the year-weeks and the years and the jubilees: there are forty-nine jubilees from the days of Adam until this day, and one week and two years: and there are yet forty years to come lit. 'distant' for learning the commandments of the Lord, until they pass over into the land of Canaan, crossing the Jordan to the ⁵west. And the jubilees shall pass by, until Israel is cleansed from all guilt of fornication, and uncleanness, and pollution, and sin, and error, and dwells with confidence in all the land, and there shall be no more a Satan or any evil one, and the land shall be clean from that time for evermore. ⁶And behold the commandment regarding the Sabbaths -I have written them down for thee- ⁷and all the judgments of its laws. Six days shalt thou labour, but on the seventh day is the Sabbath of the Lord your God. In it ye shall do no manner of work, ye and your sons, and your men-⁸servants and your maid-servants, and all your cattle and the sojourner also who is with you. And the man that does any work on it shall die: whoever desecrates that day, whoever lies with his wife, or whoever says he will do something on it, that he will set out on a journey thereon in regard to any buying or selling: and whoever draws water thereon which he had not prepared for himself on the sixth day, and whoever takes up any burden to carry it out of his tent or out of his house ⁹shall die. Ye shall do no work whatever on the Sabbath day save what ye have prepared for yourselves on the sixth day, so as to eat, and drink, and rest, and keep Sabbath from all work on that day, and to bless the Lord your God, who has given you a day of festival and a holy day: and ¹⁰a day of the holy kingdom for all Israel is this day among their days for ever. For great is the honour which the Lord has given to Israel that they should eat and drink and be satisfied on this festival day, and rest thereon from all labour which belongs to the labour of the children of men save burning frankincense and bringing oblations and sacrifices before the Lord for days and for ¹¹Sabbaths. This work alone shall be done on the Sabbath-days in the sanctuary of the Lord your God; that they may atone for Israel with sacrifice continually from day to day for a memorial well-pleasing before the Lord, and that He may receive them always from day to day according as thou ¹²hast been commanded. And every man who does any work thereon, or goes a journey, or tills his farm, whether in his house or any other place, and whoever lights a fire, or rides on any beast, or travels by ship on the sea, and whoever strikes or kills anything, or slaughters a beast or a bird, or ¹³whoever catches

an animal or a bird or a fish, or whoever fasts or makes war on the Sabbaths: The man who does any of these things on the Sabbath shall die, so that the children of Israel shall observe the Sabbaths according to the commandments regarding the Sabbaths of the land, as it is written in the tablets, which He gave into my hands that I should write out for thee the laws of the seasons, and the seasons according to the division of their days.

Herewith is completed the account of the division of the days.

www.ingramcontent.com/pod-product-compliance
Lightning Source LLC
Chambersburg PA
CBHW032143040426
42449CB00005B/377